Maryland's Public Gardens & Parks

Barbara Glickman

Schiffer Publishing Ltd
4880 Lower Valley Road • Atglen, PA 19310

Designed by John P. Cheek
Cover design by Brenda McCallum
Photographs by Barbara Glickman

Type set in Cylburn/Adobe Garamond Pro
ISBN: 978-0-7643-4920-1

Printed in China

Published by Schiffer Publishing, Ltd.
4880 Lower Valley Road
Atglen, PA 19310
Phone: (610) 593-1777; Fax: (610) 593-2002
E-mail: Info@schifferbooks.com

For our complete selection of fine books on this and related subjects, please visit our website at www.schifferbooks.com. You may also write for a free catalog.

This book may be purchased from the publisher. Please try your bookstore first.

We are always looking for people to write books on new and related subjects. If you have an idea for a book, please contact us at proposals@schifferbooks.com.

Schiffer Publishing's titles are available at special discounts for bulk purchases for sales promotions or premiums. Special editions, including personalized covers, corporate imprints, and excerpts can be created in large quantities for special needs. For more information, contact the publisher.

As someone whose earliest memories are of digging in the backyard, this book is dedicated to those who get their hands dirty working in the garden and to those who like to visit gardens.

Contents

As a sequel to her successful book *Capital Splendor: Gardens and Parks of Washington, DC*, garden writer Barbara Glickman looks to her own state of Maryland to celebrate its special and diverse public gardens. For many Marylanders, knowing and loving nature is about protecting the health of the Chesapeake Bay. When the campaign to "Save the Bay" became a concern not only about what flows from large industries and utilities' outflow pipes and smokestacks, but also about what flows from everyone's backyard, Maryland's public gardens became important laboratories and demonstrations of land stewardship. They are places to learn about native plants, rain gardens, pollinator gardens, native meadows, and alternatives to lawn. Maryland's public gardens have responded to the public's need to know.

While addressing some of the most challenging environmental concerns, these gardens open their doors every day to people of all ages to enjoy a respite from hectic lives and to be nourished by the beauty

of plants. Maryland is blessed with a diversity of plant life with the intersection of the three regions: coastal, piedmont, and mountain. It boasts northern and southern plants as their ranges reach into the mid-Atlantic. And from its colonial history until today, with new arboreta being established on college and university campuses, its gardens reflect the mores and ways of the past as well as modern tastes and sensibilities. Within a day's drive in Maryland you can discover a collection of some of the world's finest modern sculpture, internationally acclaimed topiary, a pristine colonial garden steeped in the state capital's history, a popular horticulture display garden for every season, conservatories, and estate gardens reflecting the passions, talents, and resources of their owners.

Barbara Glickman's new book highlights a public gardening world often lost between beloved Monticello and Washington, DC's Georgetown estate gardens to the south and west and Longwood Gardens to the north. Maryland's public gardens are a world that deserves to be discovered and *Maryland's Public Gardens & Parks* is your reliable guide to this adventure where you will find something for everyone. Delight and awe is an everyday occurrence at these sites.

Ellie Altman
Executive Director
Adkins Arboretum

Acknowledgments

I owe thanks to Schiffer Publishing for supporting my idea for the book and putting it into print.

I am grateful to the many garden, park, historic home, museum, and fort directors who gave me permission to take photographs to be used in the book. I also want to thank them and their staffs and volunteers for their help identifying some of the plants and for reviewing the narratives and captions for accuracy.

I especially want to thank Ellie Altman, executive director of the Adkins Arboretum, and Emily Emerick, executive director of Ladew Topiary Gardens, who provided initial support for the project and without which the project may not have gone forward.

I also want to thank Melissa Grim, chief horticulturist, and Gwen Burrell, public information officer, Baltimore City Department of Recreation and Parks; Kate Blom, supervisor, and Ann Green, volunteer coordinator, Howard Peters Rawlings Conservatory & Botanic Gardens; Jennifer Forrence, head gardener, Cylburn Arboretum; Mollie Ridout, director of horticulture, Historic Annapolis, Inc.; Rod Cofield, executive director, and Nate Powers, director of horticulture, Historic London Town and Gardens; Jay Myers, statewide volunteer coordinator and garden manager, Helen Avalynne Tawes Garden; Nancy L. Easterling, executive director, and Bob Aldridge and Daphne McGuire, Garden Guild volunteers, Sotterley Plantation; JoAnn Heard, manager of Oxon Hill Manor, The Maryland-National Capital Park and Planning Commission; Ruby Abrams, public affairs and marketing, Prince George's County Parks and Recreation; Edward Day, director, Amanda Helin, gardener, and Ann Wass, PhD, history/museum specialist, Riversdale House Museum, The Maryland-National Capital Park and Planning Commission; Andrew Banasik, director of Natural & Cultural Resources, and Brett Spaulding, park ranger, Monocacy National Battlefield; Diana Ogilvie, volunteer coordinator, and Jennifer Hill, park ranger, Patuxent Research Refuge; Susan Klise, administrator, Glenview Mansion; Rob Orndorff, horticulturist, City of Rockville; Leslie McDermott, marketing and media relations manager, Phil Normandy, plant collections manager, and Priscilla E. Taylor, program and facility manager, Brookside Gardens; Stacey Hann-Ruff, executive director, Annmarie Sculpture Garden & Arts Center; Paige Howard, executive director, and Friends of Mount Harmon, Mount Harmon Plantation; Paul Bitzel, former chief horticulturist, Hampton National Historic Site and Fort McHenry National Monument and Historic Shrine; Susan Wilkinson, director of communications and marketing, Historic St. Mary's City; Kay MacIntosh, director of media relations, Rosemary Ford, associate professor of biology, and Chris Rainer, groundskeeper, Washington College; Elena Bode, ranger, Southern Maryland Recreational Complex, Maryland Department of Natural Resources; James Abbott, director and curator, Evergreen Museum & Library; Deborah Landau, PhD, conservation ecologist, The Nature Conservancy, Maryland/DC Chapter; Karen Jarboe, Merkle crew supervisor, Merkle Wildlife Sanctuary; Lisa Alexander, executive director, Audubon Naturalist Society; Michele Whitbeck, volunteer coordinator, Blackwater National Wildlife Refuge; Stephanie Jacob and Greg Kearns, naturalists, Patuxent River Park; Julie Super, park naturalist, Meadowside Nature Center, Montgomery Parks; Meghan Sochowski, ranger, Assateague State Park; Mary Jurkiewicz, museum director, Holly Burnham, director of education, and Ann Wagner, office administrator, Montpelier Mansion, The Maryland-National Capital Park and Planning Commission; Ranger Donnie Oates, park manager, Herrington Manor/Swallow Falls State Parks; Andrew Brown, senior naturalist, Battle Creek Cypress Swamp;

Barbara Curtis, public relations and communications coordinator, Ladew Topiary Gardens; Melissa Chotiner, media relations manager, Montgomery Parks, The Maryland-National Capital Park and Planning Commission; Emily Hewitt, volunteer coordinator, and Rebecca Jameson, park ranger, Palisades District, Great Falls Tavern Visitor Center; Dave Powell, park manager, Seneca Creek State Park; Deborah Cohen, park ranger, Antietam National Battlefield; Ann Mannix-Brown, communications director, and Brad Pudner, director of landscape, Baltimore Museum of Art, and the Maryland Department of Natural Resources for allowing use of a map. I also want to thank my friends, Carol Pendás Whitten, who generously gave of her time to review the manuscript, Vicky Taplin, who reviewed the proposal, and Lori Keenan, who provided support and companionship on a trip that hinted at bears and only delivered snakes. And once again I want to thank my husband, Gary, for technical support.

Introduction

In 1927, a *National Geographic* reporter visited Maryland and gave it the nickname "America in Miniature" for a very good reason: even though it is the ninth smallest state with approximately 10,500 square miles of land and water, almost all types of natural features can be found here. Since that time, tourism officials have proudly used the moniker to publicize the state's wide-ranging attributes. The terrain ranges from sand dunes on the Eastern Shore to rolling hills in the central Piedmont Region to the Appalachian Mountains in the west. There is even a bog in western Maryland formed during the Ice Age, a phenomenon more typically found in Canada or New England! The diverse topography generates a great variety of plant life, producing an abundance of beautiful gardens and many natural or untamed parks. The natural attractions and variety of magnificent gardens reflect the state's grandeur.

Maryland has a world-class city, Baltimore, and is near another, Washington, DC, and both have first-rate museums, theater, and other cultural attractions. Naturally, their physical attributes and cultural richness have attracted a diverse population who have created and sought splendor in their gardens and parks as well, enriching them for all to enjoy. Unlike Europe with its many large and intact renowned gardens from landed gentry centuries ago, Maryland's historic gardens have been greatly reduced in size and now are often a hint of their original great estates.

In my first book, *Capital Splendor: Gardens and Parks of Washington, DC*, I included the extraordinary Ladew Topiary Gardens. Its founder, Harvey Ladew, was a transplanted New Yorker who moved to Maryland in the 1920s so that he would have more open space in which to pursue his hobby of fox hunting, and he came to love the state and its countryside. As a transplanted New Yorker who loves her adopted state, I identify with him as I have been able to pursue my interest in traveling and finding new places to explore, either by car, foot, or bicycle; the state is small and distant places are no more than a three- and-a-half hour car drive. My favorite hobby is road biking and exploring new scenic roads or areas. While biking the glorious rolling countryside near Antietam National Battlefield, I discovered Gathland State Park, which sits atop South Mountain; from there, it is just a short distance to the even more breathtaking scenery of the Middletown Valley.

As one of the original colonies, Maryland is rich in American history and many of its historic homes feature gardens, allowing visitors to learn about the history and horticulture of the time. Historic St. Mary's City is the best preserved site of a seventeenth-century English colony and the site of the state's first capital; it features gardens that demonstrate an early technique of companion gardening, known as the Three Sisters Garden, and crops used for food and medicine. Historic London Town in Edgewater was founded in 1683 and became an important tobacco port, reaching its peak in the 1720s and disappearing by the mid-1700s; its several historical gardens feature plants grown at that time, both by the colonists and by the African-American slaves. The William Paca House and Garden was built in Annapolis in the 1760s by one of the signers of the Declaration of Independence. It has plants typical of the eighteenth century, and the house tour provides information about the customs of that time. The federal-style Riversdale House Museum in Riverdale was built in the early 1800s and owned by Rosalie and her husband George Calvert, a member of Maryland's founding family; a tour of the house and garden provides insight into the operation of a large plantation around the time of the War of 1812. The Evergreen Museum & Library in Baltimore features an exceptional mid-nineteenth century Gilded Age mansion with

Italian-style gardens. These are among the many homes and gardens described in the book.

Many different types of ornamental gardens are also featured in this book, including the Howard Peters Rawlings Conservatory & Botanic Garden in Baltimore, the second-oldest steel-frame-and-glass building still in use in the country. It houses many epiphytes, such as orchids and bromeliads, desert plants, and palm trees. Another wonderful garden in Baltimore is the Cylburn Arboretum, with its formal rose garden, dahlias, woodland gardens, and others. Similarly, Brookside Gardens in Wheaton has many distinct garden areas, including a Japanese-style garden, conservatories with large tropical plants, azalea gardens, trial gardens, and others. In contrast, Adkins Arboretum on the Eastern Shore in Ridgely features the region's native plants on its 400 acres that traverse meadows, streams, and wooded forests. The sculpture gardens at the Baltimore Museum of Art and the Ann Marie Sculpture Garden & Arts Center in Solomons present sculpture in naturalistic wooded environments with many perennials and flowering shrubs. On a college campus, the Virginia Gent Decker Arboretum at Washington College has over 700 trees labeled, representing ninety species. And lastly, Maryland is home to one of the most outstanding topiary gardens in the world, the aforementioned Ladew Topiary Gardens.

The federal, state, and regional governments manage spectacular properties encompassing beautiful natural attractions. I discovered Wye Island Natural Resources Management Area in Queenstown while researching this book, and it is now a favorite of mine. I even ventured out alone to hike a trail on the first day of hunting season; the arching limbs of the Osage orange trees that enveloped me the entire way to the peaceful water's edge removed any fear of flying bullets. The tranquil sounds of swaying cattails and the gurgling of spatterdock and wild rice in the marshes at Patuxent River Park are memorable. Equally unforgettable is the stillness of the tidal marsh at Blackwater National Wildlife Refuge, save for the sounds of the slow steps of the great egrets fishing in the shallow waters. And one of my favorite roads to bike is a scenic stretch of the Chesapeake & Ohio Canal National Historic Park near Antietam National Battlefield. Maryland's wealth of natural attractions and varied topographies can accommodate people who like the shore, rolling hills, or mountains.

You will find that many historic homes with gardens are clustered near the major cities of Annapolis, Baltimore, and Washington, DC. Three remarkable historic homes in Prince George's County (Oxon Hill Manor, Riversdale House Museum, and Montpelier Mansion) have outstanding gardens, and you can tour the houses as well. Also included are two historic forts, Fort McHenry and Fort Washington, that served to protect our nation's waterways, as well as two national Civil War battlefields, Antietam and Monocacy. Two sites in western Maryland owned by The Nature Conservancy,

Finzel and Cranesville swamps, are included because of their unique plant life, and Battle Creek Cypress Swamp in southern Maryland was chosen because of its bald cypress trees. Throughout Maryland there are gardens, regional parks, state parks, wildlife refuges, natural resource management areas, tidewater plantation houses, and museum gardens waiting to be explored.

Over thirty of the sites feature water, including the Potomac River, Patuxent River, and Chesapeake Bay, as well as lesser known rivers such as the Wye, South, Blackwater, and Sassafras. Some state parks, such as Rocky Gap and Deep Creek, and Black Hills Regional Park were selected because of their stunning lakes, all providing majestic scenery and outstanding recreational opportunities. None of Maryland's lakes are natural since glaciers did not go as far south as Maryland to carve out deep lakes. Yet they are extremely scenic, often surrounded by lush forests with minimal development.

Some of the gardens featured are representative of or include elements of certain garden styles. The garden at Montpelier Mansion is representative of a colonial garden, with a picket fence, boxwood, herbs, and practical and ornamental flowers, all enclosed by an outer worm or zigzag fence. Among the many garden areas at Brookside Gardens is a Japanese-style garden, with a gazebo, stepping stones, and pond. A Japanese-style bridge is found at the William Paca Garden. Parterres, whose origin is French, are at the William Paca Garden and Hampton National Historic Site. The garden at Evergreen Museum & Library had an Italian-style grotto, but it is now somewhat filled in.

In the book, gardens and parks are organized by county and it is certainly possible to visit several in a day. The map in the front of the book will assist in trip planning, and the information in the back provides basic information, such as address and phone for each site.

My original plan for the book started with forty-four sites but it quickly grew to fifty-two. Obviously, there are many more sites with magnificent scenery and worthy of inclusion, but the book would have been much longer and so the sites chosen are personal. The eight Maryland gardens in *Capital Splendor* are included as well, for to exclude them would be unacceptable. Nearly twenty of the fifty-two gardens were new to me, as I first discovered them while researching the book and was thrilled to find and visit them.

Go spend the next year visiting one a week, learning about the history and enjoying the gardens and natural attractions that make diverse Maryland "America in Miniature."

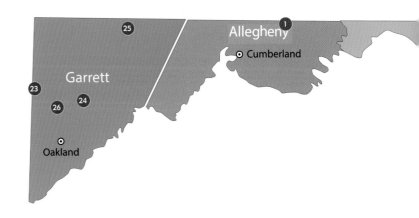

Map of Maryland's Gardens and Parks

1 Rocky Gap State Park
2 Helen Avalynne Tawes Garden
3 Historic London Town and Gardens
4 William Paca House and Garden
5 Baltimore Museum of Art Sculpture Garden
6 Cylburn Arboretum
7 Evergreen Museum & Library
8 Fort McHenry National Monument and Historic Shrine
9 Howard Peters Rawlings Conservatory & Botanic Gardens of Baltimore
10 Sherwood Gardens
11 Hampton National Historic Site
12 Annmarie Sculpture Garden & Arts Center
13 Battle Creek Cypress Swamp
14 Calvert Cliffs State Park
15 Mount Harmon Plantation
16 Chapman State Park
17 Blackwater National Wildlife Refuge

18 Cunningham Falls State Park
19 Gathland State Park
20 Monocacy National Battlefield
21 Sugarloaf Mountain
22 Washington Monument State Park
23 Cranesville Swamp
24 Deep Creek Lake State Park
25 Finzel Swamp
26 Swallow Falls State Park
27 Ladew Topiary Gardens
28 Brighton Dam Azalea Garden
29 Audubon Naturalist Society
30 Black Hill Regional Park
31 Brookside Gardens
32 Cabin John Regional Park
33 Chesapeake & Ohio Canal National Historic Park
34 Glenview Mansion
35 McCrillis Gardens

36 McKee-Beshers Wildlife Management Area
37 Rock Creek Regional Park
38 Seneca Creek State Park
39 Fort Washington Park
40 Merkle Wildlife Sanctuary
41 Montpelier Mansion
42 Oxon Hill Manor
43 Patuxent Research Refuge
44 Patuxent River Park
45 Riversdale House Museum
46 Adkins Arboretum
47 The Washington College Virginia Gent Decker Arboretum
48 Wye Island Natural Resources Management Area
49 Historic St. Mary's City
50 Sotterley Plantation
51 Antietam National Battlefield
52 Assateague State Park

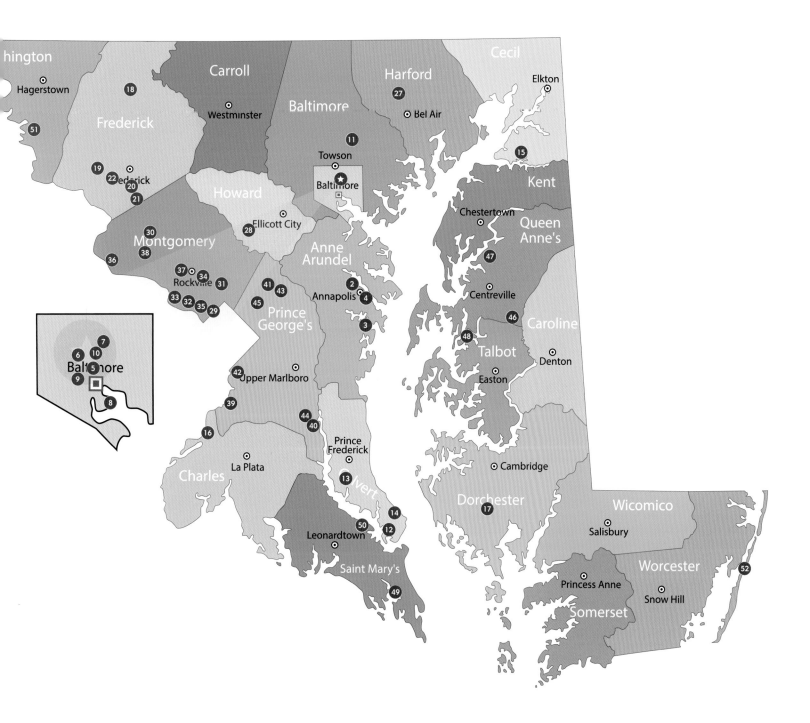

hington

Hagerstown ⊙

18 ⊙

Carroll

Frederick

51 ⊙

Westminster ⊙

Cecil

Elkton ⊙

Harford

27 ⊙

⊙ Bel Air

Baltimore

11 ⊙

19 ⊙
22 ⊙ Frederick
20 ⊙
21 ⊙

Howard

Towson ⊙

★ Baltimore ⊙

15 ⊙

Kent

30 ⊙
Montgomery
38 ⊙

36 ⊙

Ellicott City ⊙
28 ⊙

Chestertown ⊙

Queen
Anne's

37 ⊙ 34
Rockville
33 ⊙ 32 ⊙ 35 ⊙ 29
31

41 ⊙ 43
45 ⊙

Anne
Arundel

2 ⊙
Annapolis ⊙ 4

47 ⊙

Centreville ⊙

7 ⊙
6 ⊙ 10
Baltimore
5
9 ⊙ ⊙
8

Prince
George's

3 ⊙

46 ⊙

Caroline

48 ⊙

Talbot

Denton ⊙

42 ⊙ Upper Marlboro ⊙

Easton ⊙

39 ⊙

16 ⊙

La Plata ⊙

44 ⊙
40

Prince
Frederick ⊙

Cambridge ⊙

Charles

Calvert

13 ⊙

14 ⊙

Dorchester

17 ⊙

Wicomico

Salisbury ⊙

50 ⊙
12

Leonardtown ⊙

Saint Mary's

49 ⊙

Worcester

52 ⊙

Princess Anne ⊙

Snow Hill ⊙

Somerset

15

The park offers two swimming beaches and a third one at the campsite.

1. Rocky Gap State Park

Rocky Gap State Park is a picturesque 3,400-acre park set amid the mountains of Allegheny County. It features a lake and watersports, many hiking trails, a campground, nature center, aviary, and many pavilions and an amphitheater.

The idea for the park originated with Edward Habeeb, for whom the lake is named. He was president of the Route 40 Association, an organization whose mission was to promote business and industry in Allegheny County by improving highways and establishing a park. He donated land for the park and encouraged many others to do so, and the park opened to the public in 1974. The park includes a cemetery from the 1800s with several Civil War era stones, which is open to visitors.

The 243-acre Lake Habeeb, like all Maryland lakes, is man-made and was formed by building a dam to confine Rocky Gap Run. It has several beach areas, and boat rentals allow one to further explore and appreciate the beauty of the setting. A four-and-a-half-mile Lakeside Trail rewards one with views of the lake and woodlands filled with rhododendron and mountain laurel. A short hike through rhododendron and a hemlock forest provides views of the one-mile gorge with its sheer cliffs. The five-mile Evitt's Homesite Trail goes through a hemlock forest and offers impressive views with its 1,000-foot elevation.

Boating on Lake Habeeb is a good way to enjoy all the beautiful mountain scenery.

Anne Arundel County

Violet rhododendron and yellow irises provide seasonal color near the wooded stream, an ecosystem representative of central Maryland.

2. Helen Avalynne Tawes Garden

Located away from the normal tourist sites in Annapolis is the pleasant five acre Helen Avalynne Tawes Garden, dedicated in honor of the wife of Governor J. Millard Tawes. The present garden had been a flat cinder lot adjacent to the Tawes Building, built in the late 1960s to house the Maryland Department of Natural Resources. In 1973, an active member of the Federated Garden Clubs of Maryland advocated for a garden that would have a handicapped accessible trail with a "Maryland-in-Miniature" theme. The garden received a Design Excellence award from the American Society of Landscape Architects in 1982 and in 2013 achieved Arboretum status.

The three distinct geographical regions of Maryland are represented, including an Eastern Shore peninsula, a western Maryland forest, and a streamside environment typical of central Maryland. A blending of native and non-native plants from each habitat are featured and often labeled. Visitors entering the garden can experience a path winding around a large pond surrounded by an abundance of yellow flag irises in the spring. The various ponds are home to mallard ducks, painted turtles, assorted fish, and bullfrogs. Further along the pathway, colorful varieties of rhododendron and azaleas, as well as ferns and evergreens, make an impressive show in late spring. The garden is designed with numerous benches and seating areas to encourage visitors to relax and savor the views. An area called the Plant Mural under a semicircular arbor always has seasonal interest with its perennials, annuals, and shrubs.

Yellow irises and yellowwood trees line the banks of the pond in springtime.

Ducks enjoy the beauty and serenity of the garden.

The 'Sappho' rhododendron, one of many varieties planted in the garden, has white flowers with a conspicuous dark purple blotch.

The white flowers of the yellowwood tree are very fragrant and they form wisteria-like clusters.

German bearded iris, sedum 'Autumn Joy', and red hot poker are some of the many annuals, perennials, and shrubs on display showcasing what the average gardener can plant in his own garden.

Peonies, with the South River in the background, make a magnificent scene.

3. Historic London Town and Gardens

Perfectly combining history, gardens, and archaeology, the twenty-three-acre Historic London Town and Gardens is situated on an idyllic setting along the South River in Edgewater, near Annapolis. The gardens include native plants and some uncommon specimens not generally found in gardens in this region. The site is owned by Anne Arundel County and is operated by the London Town Foundation. The William Brown house on the property was listed as a National Historic Landmark in 1970.

The 100-acre London Town was an important tobacco port with a population of 300 to 400 people at its peak in the 1720s. However, trade diminished during the Revolutionary War; as Annapolis and Baltimore became important cities, London Town slowly disappeared. The imposing large Georgian house called the William Brown house was built about 1760 and is the sole remaining building. Anne Arundel County purchased the house and ten acres to use as an almshouse in 1828. Following the passage of the 1965 National Welfare Act, the site became a county park. The original buildings from the seventeenth and eighteenth centuries are being researched by archaeologists from the Anne Arundel County Lost Towns Project, and one dwelling, the Lord Mayor's Tenement, has been accurately reconstructed.

Development of the gardens began in the late 1960s as a cooperative venture among local garden clubs, county officials, the University of Maryland, and interested individuals. The three main garden areas are the eight-acre Woodland Garden, the Ornamental Gardens, and the Historic Gardens. The gardens are still evolving, with plans for a Children's Sensory Garden and a Waterside Native Plant Trail. Special overlooks and memorial areas dot the entire garden area.

The Woodland Garden consists mainly of garden "rooms," each of which has a specified botanical collection, mixing native plants with exotics from the same species. The Woodland Garden "rooms" have many varieties of holly trees, camellias, azaleas, and magnolias. Occasionally, a "room" also has a rare specimen, such as evergreen dogwood (*Cornus capitata*), with red fruit and green leaves providing rich color in fall and winter. Views of South River and Almshouse Creek and the aquatic plants and grasses add beauty and excitement to the garden during all seasons.

Over 200 cultivars of camellias are planted along the Camellia Walk, and in other "room" locations. Largely the 1978–1980 project of William

Ackerman, PhD, of the United States National Arboretum, who sought to breed cold hardy hybrid fall-, winter-, and spring-blooming camellias, this inviting path is purposely close to the cool breezes from the South River. Parallel to the Camellia Walk, the Winter Walk provides sensory stimulation during all seasons, with an abundance of color afforded by foliage, flowers, berries, or dazzling bark of trees. Color comes from the white, pink, and red flowers of camellias, yellow and orange flowers of witch hazel, hellebores of all colors in spring, hydrangeas in summer, and viburnums in spring and fall. Many plants, such as daphne and wintersweet, give off a heady aroma in winter.

Purple irises and verbena are in beds by the gazebo.

Steps leading up to the Woodland Garden are lined with azaleas, ferns, and heliotropes.

The William Brown House is a large Georgian-style house overlooking the South River. Constructed using a header bond bricklaying technique, which was both expensive and fashionable, the house was used as an upscale tavern for travelers crossing the South River by ferry.

Colorful red-veined Swiss chard, collards, and fennel are in the colonial kitchen adjacent to the two-story, two-room earthfast structure known as Lord Mayor's Tenement.

The cold-tolerant 'Snow Flurry' camellia has lush peony-like pure white blossoms.

The Ornamental Garden is best known for its peonies, and the large collection includes herbaceous, tree, and fern leaf peonies. Daffodils, cherries, daylilies, roses, hydrangeas, and many other species bloom in sequence ensuring color in this garden all year long. Exotic and native trees are found here as well, and a rare Japanese flowering apricot tree provides magnificent, spicy, fragrant red flowers in winter.

The Historical Gardens are comprised of the colonial kitchen garden and the African-American garden. Typical of colonial gardens, both are laid out in a four-square pattern with a southern exposure and are fenced with closely placed pickets. The kitchen garden provides root vegetables in winter, and beans and squash in summer. The African-American garden contains native tobacco, Maryland's former primary economic crop, along with staples such as peppers, black-eye peas, and sorghum popular with African-Americans in the colonial ara.

The two-story summer house is the focal point at the end of the gravel path that bisects the garden. The dome of the Naval Academy Chapel is in the background.

4. William Paca House and Garden

The William Paca Garden is a breathtaking urban colonial pleasure garden in downtown Annapolis. A National Historic Landmark, this two-acre garden is a re-creation of Paca's original pre-Revolutionary terraced garden. The quaint brick sidewalks and narrow streets of Annapolis provide a hint of the unique garden behind the William Paca house.

William Paca was a signer of the Declaration of Independence, a Revolutionary-era governor of Maryland, and a prominent lawyer. The house was built between 1763 and 1765, and the garden he designed during the fifteen years that he lived there was one of the most remarkable in the affluent town. Paca's garden was unique in that it incorporated both formal and natural styles that were common in England at that time.

The estate was sold in 1780 and fell into decline during the next century. In the early 1900s, the garden was torn up and then covered with nine feet of earth to make way for a 200-room hotel called Carvel Hall. In the 1960s and 1970s, Historic Annapolis Foundation rescued the property and the state of Maryland purchased it. Through archaeological excavations and artwork showing William Paca standing in his garden, landscape architects were able to re-create the garden, which opened to the public in 1973. The mission of the garden is to preserve rare and antique plant species that were grown 300 years ago in the Annapolis area.

The garden is divided into two sections: the formal ones closer to the house and the "wilderness" in the far back. A few fragments remained of the distinctive brick walls with their narrow vertical slits that have now been rebuilt and enclose the garden. The upper terrace, closest to the house, was intended for entertaining and viewing, and is still used for social occasions. The four terraces, typical of a Chesapeake falling garden, are laid out in parterres that provide seasonal color and texture. Beds of heirloom roses form the geometric pattern on the west side and flowers grown in Paca's time, such as spring flowering bulbs, irises, daylilies and asters, compose the flower parterre on the east side. Go down a few steps to the next parterre that has American hollies pruned into conical shapes, and across the way is the boxwood parterre. A kitchen garden of seasonal vegetables, including pole beans, peppers, and squash, is also on the eastern end near the flower parterre. Down the next set of steps is the orchard, with cordoned apple and plum trees, and pear trees trained into an overhead arch. The garden is especially fragrant, as the arbors are covered with wisteria and double musk rose. Benches in the parterres allow for a leisurely visit. "Necessaries" (or privies) at each end of the garden now serve as tool sheds.

The natural landscape or "wilderness" area is reached by crossing the small canal and then crossing the Chinese latticework bridge over the fish-shaped pond, with a large bald cypress towering over it. Paw paws, buckeye, fringe trees, and other species native to the mid-Atlantic are found throughout this section. The focal point of the rear of the garden is the two-story summer house, which was used as a retreat and as a viewpoint for the garden or the world beyond the high brick walls. Other noteworthy buildings at the back of the garden are the spring house in the northwest corner and the bath house in the northeast corner.

Looking toward the house, the fish shape of the pond is easily discernible. A natural spring in the spring house feeds the pond.

An arbor of pear trees is in the foreground of the holly parterre.

The flower parterre, divided into eight geometric beds around a center, provides three seasons of bloom. All the flowers were cultivated during William Paca's time.

The damask rose is one of the several heirloom roses in the rose parterre. These ancient varieties bloom only once a season and the damask rose is very fragrant and has many thorns. It was cultivated for perfume in ancient times.

Above:
Emile-Antoine Bourdelle's *Fruit* is set among Boston ivy and near a dwarf cut-leaf Japanese maple tree.

Right:
Daffodils herald springtime and the start of the succession of blooms in the Ryda and Robert H. Levi Sculpture Garden naturalistic garden.

Far right:
A blackhaw viburnum and 'Delaware Valley White' azaleas provide the backdrop for Auguste Rodin's *Nude Honoré de Balzac with Folded Arms.*

5. Baltimore Museum of Art
Sculpture Garden

The geometric abstraction of *The Horse*, by Raymond Duchamp-Villon, is set among daffodils in the Alan and Janet Wurzburger Sculpture Garden.

The Baltimore Museum of Art Sculpture Garden is a perfect complement to the museum's collection of modern and contemporary art. The nearly three-acre garden consists of two terraced areas: The Wurtzburger Sculpture Garden and the Ryda and Robert H. Levi Sculpture Garden. Mature trees, flowering bulbs, and colorful shrubs enhance the many vistas of the sculptures.

The Baltimore Museum of Art was founded in 1914 and opened in its current location in 1929 with a building designed by the famous American architect John Russell Pope. In addition to having the largest collection of art by Henri Matisse, other outstanding collections include European masterpieces, African art, abstract expressionism, and the Cone Collection with works by Cézanne, Matisse, Gauguin, van Gogh, and others.

The Wurtzburger Sculpture Garden opened in 1980 and approximately twenty of its thirty-five major pieces are on display at any time, ranging from August Rodin's *Balzac* to works by Henry Moore. The design includes flagstone pathways and springtime daffodils and tulips, echoing the garden design of Alan and Janet Wurtzburger's estate in Baltimore. The real estate investor and his wife collected African, Pacific Island, and Ancient American art, in addition to nineteenth-century and contemporary sculpture. White flowers are used in abundance to highlight the sculptures. August Rodin's *Nude Honoré de Balzac with Folded Arms* is set amid a show of continuously blooming white flowers, from azaleas to astilbe to hydrangea. For year-round interest there are shrubs with texture and winter color, such as linden viburnum with their red berries.

A lower terrace of nearly two acres comprises the Ryda and Robert H. Levi Sculpture Garden, which opened in 1988 and has approximately twenty sculptures. Ryda Hecht Levi was a philanthropist, and her husband, Robert, was a businessman and banker. Artists from the second half of the twentieth century are represented, including Joan Miró and Alexander Calder. Poplar, ash, American beech trees, and a wisteria arbor provide shade and privacy and act as a backdrop for the sculptures to shine. The Levis wanted to maintain the naturalistic urban park, similar to their own garden. Plants provide a succession of colorful blooms throughout the year, with daffodils in early spring, Siberian and Japanese irises later, and in late fall, the red berries of nandina and the purple berries of the beauty berry. Planted ferns aid in water control and prevent erosion.

Weeping higan cherry trees provide a glorious background for two Lady Baltimore statues in the formal garden. On the statues are symbols of Baltimore's major industries of shipping, health, and manufacturing, represented by an anchor, caduceus, and gear.

6. Cylburn Arboretum

Cylburn Arboretum is a magnificent 207-acre oasis within the city limits of Baltimore, featuring formal and display gardens, a large collection of trees and shrubs, and woodland trails. Although the garden is not far from downtown Baltimore, it has an absolute country feel to it.

The Victorian mansion on the property was built as a summerhouse in the 1860s by Jesse Tyson, the president of Baltimore Chrome Works. Its distinctive architectural features include a mansard roof and Italianate-style cupola atop the tower. Other aspects that lend appeal to the opulent mansion are the plantings along the perimeter of the house, the lion statuary on the mansion's porch, and the circular driveway. In 1954, a city park called the Cylburn Wildflower Preserve and Garden Center was created on the grounds. Then it was developed into a horticulture and environmental education center with trails and gardens planned by volunteers. Nearly thirty years later, the park was given the name Cylburn Arboretum, and in 2010, the Vollmer Center, a visitor and education center, opened. The Horticultural Division of the Baltimore City Department of Recreation and Parks administers it.

Approximately twenty different gardens are displayed. Formal Victorian-designed gardens east of the mansion are approached through a path guarded over by a set of lion statues. Two Lady Baltimore statues preside over the tranquil garden, undoubtedly preferring their beautiful setting to their former perch on one of the bridges over St. Paul Street. This is a popular site for weddings. Elsewhere, a Garden of the Senses features waist-high flowering plants and shrubs so that those physically challenged can smell and feel them. Other gardens feature dahlias, vegetables, and heritage roses. Tyson's estate plantings are the basis for the shrubs and trees on site, which include magnolias, boxwood, conifers, Japanese maples, and hollies. From the gazebo, one can admire the amazing array of color in the perennial garden or view the extensive open rolling grounds or the mansion. Two and a half miles of trails winding through the woodland provide a home to native and migrating birds. A nature museum houses a collection of butterflies, moths, and birds.

Waving Shirley poppies and silky Mexican feather grass are inviting in the Worthley Garden near the front of the house.

Right:
The opulent mansion is surrounded by beautiful gardens on all sides. The spiky plant in front is an *Allium schubertii*, behind it is a 'Golden Sword' yucca, while the plant with feathery plumes is a Mexican feather grass, and the succulent, on the bottom right, is donkey tail spurge.

Far right:
A garden of dahlias is just one of the many special garden areas.

The lavender on the left is Spanish lavender (*Lavandula stoechas*), and it is pineapple-shaped with tufts that look like rabbit ears.

The foxtail lilies (*Eremurus bungei*) have fantastic flower spikes that look like large candles or the animal's tail.

The formal garden has 'Knock Out' roses, a sundial, and the two Lady Baltimore statues watching over it.

The stunning cinnamon-colored bark of the river birch tree peels off into thin curls, enhancing its beauty.

Statuary, terraces, a grotto, and manicured boxwood are featured in the Italian-style formal upper garden.

Mature trees in the park-like entrance lawn project a pastoral view, a concept espoused by landscape architect Frederick Law Olmsted.

A grotto was created in 1935 by carving an archway in the wall. Formal garden design was fashionable at the time, so the gardens were altered and an Italian design was adapted.

7. Evergreen Museum & Library

Evergreen Museum & Library is a glorious example of an Italianate mansion from the Gilded Age. Outstanding architectural features include the Corinthian portico, the cupola, and the ornate cornices. The house and gardens occupy twenty-six acres just north of downtown Baltimore, and the house is listed on the National Register of Historic Places. The house and its collections have been under the custodianship of the Johns Hopkins University since 1942.

Stephen Broadbent had the house built in 1857, but upon acquiring the house in 1878, the Garrett family made major improvements to the house and grounds until they bequeathed the property to Johns Hopkins University. In 1878, John Work Garrett, president of the Baltimore and Ohio Railroad, bought Evergreen for his son Thomas and his family. The two generations that lived there were collectors of books and art. The main library, a spectacular room overlooking the gardens, contains a collection of natural history books, including a pristine set of John James Audubon's double-elephant folio *Birds of America*, autographs by every signer of the Declaration of Independence but one, and original works by Shakespeare. The house contains one of the largest private collections of Louis Comfort Tiffany art glass and many paintings by artists such as Modigliani, Degas, Picasso, Bonnard, and Vuillard. In addition, ceilings, columns, and walls in the theater have stenciled designs by Léon Bakst, the Russian-émigré set designer and artist.

The design for the park-like front lawn with mature trees was created in consultation with the famous landscape architect Frederick Law Olmsted and others. When the house was built, naturalistic landscape design was popular, characterized by its pastoral views and asymmetrical plantings, and advocated by landscape architects such as Olmsted and Andrew Jackson Downing. However, in the early 1900s, formal garden design based on the gardens of Italian villas was becoming fashionable, so the gardens at Evergreen were adapted to that style. The gardens have changed substantially from their original design, which formerly contained greenhouses, including one for palms, and one for the tropical and exotic plants that the first generation of Garretts ordered from England and Japan. In the back, the enchanting manicured formal gardens with their classical features certainly evoke Italianate design. One feature is the grotto on the main wall, which is reminiscent of European gardens. Statuary near the grotto, rows of boxwood, a fountain at the far end of the lawn, and urns overflowing with colorful annuals, all contribute to the charm of the Italian-style garden. Beyond the formal gardens, the grounds also include an expansive meadow and stream.

Francis Scott Key was three miles out in the harbor when he saw the American flag that inspired him to write the poem that became our national anthem.

8. Fort McHenry National Monument and Historic Shrine

Fort McHenry National Monument and Historic Shrine is famous for the historic events that occurred there during the War of 1812 and inspired Francis Scott Key to compose "The Star-Spangled Banner." The melody of a popular English tune, "Anacreon in Heaven," was used for Key's lyrics, and it was not until 1931 that the song became our national anthem. Fort McHenry is on forty-two acres of the tip of a peninsula formed by two branches of the Patapsco River in Baltimore. The poignant exhibits and film on the fort's history in the Visitor Center set the stage for the stirring view of the fort and the harbor, as one could imagine the British ships out there. The fort was designated a national park in 1925 under the War Department, and redesignated a national monument and historic shrine eleven years later, the only doubly designated site in the US. In 1966, it was placed on the National Register of Historic Places.

An earthen star fort was first built on the site in 1776 in anticipation of a British attack. A series of coastal forts was authorized by Congress in 1794, so Fort McHenry, named for the second secretary of war, James McHenry, was built between 1799 and 1802. Its star shape with five bastions was based on a French design, with a dry moat encircling the fortification. The British army burned the Capitol and White House in August 1814, but then failed to capture Fort McHenry following a twenty-five-hour bombardment on September 13 and 14. The flag that was raised to signal American victory was originally thirty feet by forty-two feet. Additional earthen fortifications with larger guns were added after 1814. On the grounds is a statue titled *Orpheus with the Awkward Knee*, erected in 1922 in honor of Francis Scott Key and the military servicemen who defended Baltimore. Groves of Yoshino cherry trees and flowering crabapple in commemorative plantings can be seen from the sea wall trail that encircles the fort.

The cannons' fiery past is as radiant as the sunlit path.

Second stories and porches were added to the barracks in the 1830s.

The statue of Orpheus, a legendary musician and poet in Greek mythology, is in close proximity to the fort and is dedicated to Francis Scott Key and the fort's soldiers.

Nearly 200 Yoshino cherry trees are on the grounds of the fort.

The magnificent Palm House, listed on the National Register of Historic Places, was based on a similar structure in London's Kew Gardens.

9. Howard Peters Rawlings Conservatory & Botanic Gardens

Located in historic Druid Hill Park, the stunning Howard Peters Rawlings Conservatory and Botanic Gardens of Baltimore is one of the few outstanding Victorian conservatories intact in the world. Baltimore had four other conservatories at one time, and all were eventually demolished. The conservatory was built in 1888 and is the second-oldest steel-frame-and-glass edifice still in use in the country.

The Baltimore Conservatory Association and the City of Baltimore ardently carry out the mission of fostering an appreciation and understanding of plants from around the world and the roles they play in our lives. Information on the plants is provided throughout the rooms. The lobby features several spectacular shows during the year, including poinsettias in December, and tulips, lilies, and hyacinths that provide a colorful Easter display.

The Palm House, at fifty feet high, provides living space for very tall palm specimens, such as the Fiji, Foxtail, and the Bismarck. Public conservatories such as this were very popular for exhibiting the diverse collections of exotic plants that people brought back during worldwide voyages during the Victorian age, the second half of the 1900s. Next, the Orchid Room features in bloom a range of the more than 30,000 species of orchids that exist, as orchids constitute ten percent of the world's plant species. The next three greenhouses were added later, and they showcase plants of Mediterranean, tropical, and desert climates. Bougainvillea, oleander, and citrus trees are found in the Mediterranean space, while the Tropical House features fruit trees such as banana and flowering plants such as bird-of-paradise and passionflower. The hot and moist air, mist, and lovely fragrances, combined with the waterfall and pond containing fish and aquatic plants, will keep you lingering here awhile. Fascinating "air plants" such as bromeliads can be examined on the back wall as their aerial roots attach to tree branches. The Desert Room houses succulents, cacti, and a large agave with variegated green and yellow leaves. Thirty-five beds of flowers and plants are featured in the one and a half acres of grounds outside.

In the Tropical House, the banana tree and the other plants require warm temperatures and high humidity. The nearby shorter plant with the large pink flowers, *Megaskepasma erythrochlamys* or Brazilian red cloak, uses its huge leaves to capture light.

The Bismarck palm tree is shown, but other palms that reside in the fifty-foot high Palm House are the Fiji and European fan.

The *Agave Americana* 'Variegata' dies after it flowers, but shoots produced at its base continue to grow.

Orchids from around the world are displayed in the Orchids Room, which is part of the original conservatory.

Sherwood Garden's tulips are a highlight of Baltimore's springtime.

Colorful clusters of tulips create a spectacular show.

Tulips are the stars, but there are also boxwoods, dogwoods, azaleas, and evergreens.

Approximately 80,000 bulbs are planted every year.

10. Sherwood Gardens

With 80,000 tulip bulbs planted annually, the six-acre Sherwood Gardens in the stately residential Guilford neighborhood of North Baltimore has been called the most famous tulip garden in North America. The residents of Guilford own the garden, which is managed through Stratford Green, a nonprofit entity.

The garden is on the former 350-acre Guilford estate of A. S. Abell, founder of *The Baltimore Sun*. Around 1912, the locale was starting to get developed, and the present-day gardens, formerly situated on the site of a boat lake, were filled in. The tulip garden covers Stratford Green, one of the first parks designed by the Olmsted Brothers, the company formed by the sons of the famed landscape architect Frederick Law Olmsted. John Sherwood, an oil pioneer and resident whose house abutted Stratford Green, bought additional lots for the garden and purchased tulips from the Netherlands. He died in 1965, bequeathing funds for the continuation of the garden, and then the Guilford Association bought more lots and took responsibility for the garden. Each year, tulips are dug up and replaced, and annuals provide lots of color during the summer.

Tulips are planted in clusters around the many flowering cherry trees, dogwoods, azaleas, and magnolias, with some trees totally encircled by beds of hundreds of tulips. Magnificent beds of pink tulips near purple azaleas, and beds of white and red tulips create a wonderful kaleidoscope of colors. Mature trees and open grassy areas create the park-like setting so the real stars, the tulips, can prevail. Mr. Sherwood liked to bring back plants such as boxwood from colonial estate gardens in southern Maryland, and so some of the plants are from the eighteenth century. Benches throughout allow for a leisurely stay, and many families come with blankets, picnics, and frolicking children.

Baltimore County

The cedar of Lebanon tree on the Great Terrace is the largest in Maryland. The mansion may have been the largest private home in America when it was completed in 1790.

11. Hampton National Historic Site

Hampton National Historic Site is a stunning property due to the grandeur of the mansion, the grounds, and its history. Situated on just sixty-three acres now, it has majestic old trees, including three state champions, and beautiful historic landscaping. At its peak, the estate was one-quarter the size of present-day Baltimore!

Seven generations of the Ridgely family owned the estate, from 1745 until the mid-1900s. The first owner, Colonel Charles Ridgely, bought 11,000 acres and grew wealthy from real estate transactions, a mercantile business, agriculture, and the large ironworks he and his sons built on the estate. His son Captain Charles Ridgely expanded the landholdings to 25,000 acres; supplied arms and ammunitions during the Revolutionary War from the ironworks; cultivated grain crops and orchards, bred cattle, pigs, and horses; and owned ships that transported iron and cash crops headed for England and returned with luxury items and manufactured goods. The Ridgely businesses facilitated Baltimore's rise as a preeminent East Coast port city, and their breeding and racing of thoroughbred horses in the late 1700s fostered Maryland's role as a horse-racing hub in the early 1900s. Construction of the classic Georgian mansion, one of the largest in the country at the time, occurred between 1783 and 1790, and it is a large three-story building with wings on both sides, topped by a large octagonal cupola. The stone exterior is covered with a stucco containing iron oxide, giving the house a warm pinkish color.

Captain Ridgely's nephew and heir, Charles Carnan Ridgely, a Maryland governor, originally laid out the terraced Falling Garden. The third masters of Hampton, John and Eliza Ridgely, brought back furnishings from their travels to Europe, and Eliza imported plants and trees from Asia and the Middle East. It is thought that she brought back the cedar of Lebanon tree, now an imposing state champion on the Great Terrace, in a shoebox from a Grand Tour of the Mediterranean. Interested in horticulture, she planted exotic trees throughout the grounds, such as the empress tree and ginkgo, and ordered thirty-two marble urns to grace the mansion landscape. Eliza also planted many conifers such as white pine, hemlock, Norway spruce, and larch. She was probably influenced by Andrew Jackson Downing, the famous landscape gardener, who was a proponent of the naturalistic style. In the National Gallery of Art hangs a famous portrait of Eliza painted by Thomas Sully called *Lady with a Harp*.

Hampton's decline started after the Civil War and became critical by the Great Depression. In the mid-1940s, the family sold the property to a charitable foundation, which in turn presented it to the National Park Service. Because of its architectural significance, the mansion and forty-three acres were designated a National Historic Site in 1948.

The park-like setting of the Great Terrace, on which the mansion is situated, is filled with a collection of awe-inspiring large and old trees including Eliza Ridgely's cedar of Lebanon. There are two magnificent catalpas dating from 1774, years before the house was built. The twisted empress tree is a reminder of the timelessness of the property and the good care given it by the National Park Service. Other large trees near the mansion include a European linden tree, Canada hemlock, black walnut, gingko, and bald cypress. The pleasant walkway separating the terrace from the parterre gardens below is filled with red cedars, infusing the vista down the path and below with a tinge of Italy. European terraced gardens normally used formal stairs leading to their gardens, but the grassy ramp seen at Hampton was more commonly used in the mid-Atlantic region. The National Park Service has restored the Falling Garden to its mid-nineteenth-century design using heirloom plant material such as boxwood, spiraea, and a variety of annual bedding plants. A rare weeping Japanese pagoda tree can be found on a lower terrace near a spectacular saucer magnolia planted about 1832. West of the mansion is the Orangery, a replica of the original built around 1825, and used to overwinter citrus trees. Ruins of two historic greenhouses have been preserved. From the late 1700s to the early 1900s there were orchards on the estate with apple, pear, cherry, and peach trees. A remnant of the larger plantation can be viewed across Hampton Lane at the farm, where the historic 1745 Lower House and outbuildings, such as workers' quarters, dairy, and a mule barn, still exist.

The Red Cedar-lined pathway separates the Great Terrace from the Falling Garden with its colorful parterres.

Red wax begonias and yellow lantana are seen in Parterre I. Red and white pelargonium would have been used during Charles Carnan Ridgely's time. The weeping Japanese pagoda tree is in the background.

Blue petunias, orange marigolds and chartreuse coleus are planted in Parterre II. The Japanese fiber banana tree in the center is a cold-hardy species used to replace an Abyssinian species historically grown there.

The sculpture *A Tribute to the Oyster Tonger, A Chesapeake Waterman* is at the entrance to the garden. It was done in 1994 by Antonio Tobias Mendez in bronze and granite.

12. Annmarie Sculpture Garden
& Arts Center

The Annmarie Sculpture Garden & Arts Center is a thirty-acre sculpture garden set among forests and fields adjacent to St. John's Creek in Solomons. It is owned and supported by the Board of Calvert County Commissioners. Through exhibits, events, classes, and programs, the center's mission is to link people to nature and art.

In the mid-1950s, Washington, DC, architect and builder Francis Koenig, and his wife, Ann, bought property among the tobacco farms of Calvert County. During their frequent trips to Europe, they had seen sculpture gardens, and in 1991 they donated property to be used for this purpose. Currently, the Koenig Private Foundation operates the center, and many activities and programs are supported by Ann's Circle Inc., a nonprofit organization. When the center became a member of the Smithsonian Institution's Affiliations Program in 2003, it was able to borrow twenty-five pieces of sculpture from the Hirshhorn Museum and Sculpture Garden. The Arts Building and Studio School opened in 2001.

A paved quarter-mile path meanders through the woods, filled with more than thirty works of outdoor sculpture. Some are permanent and others are on loan, and many of them are from the Hirshhorn and the National Gallery of Art. Fairy houses placed throughout the forest add to the fun. Hundreds of Glenn Dale azaleas provide colorful accent to the sculpture, the main attraction. More than twenty types of trees can be found, including the imperial-looking loblolly pine, sassafras, Eastern red cedar, maple, and tulip poplar. A large butterfly garden of thirty-five pollinator plants adds seasonal allure.

The sculpture *After Iyengar* is named after an Indian yoga master and is set in a grassy area. It was sculpted in bronze by Robert Engman.

Along the wooded path, the sculpture *Daimaru X* is surrounded by lily of the valley plants. Michael Todd sculpted it from steel.

The ceramic entrance gates are called *The Gateway*, and were made by Peter King and Marni Jaime. They symbolize Calvert County's landscape of trees and fields at the water's edge.

Many fairy houses and gnome homes are scattered throughout the garden. Here is The Troll and the Three Billy Goats Gruff.

The bald cypress loses its needles in winter and remains bare or bald until the spring.
The knees range in height from those just protruding from the water to some that are several feet high.

13. Battle Creek Cypress Swamp

Situated in the gently rolling farmland of southern Maryland is Battle Creek Cypress Swamp, the site of one of the northernmost stands of bald cypress trees in the United States. The Nature Conservancy purchased the 100-acre preserve in 1957; it was the first preserve it purchased in Maryland. Calvert County has leased and operated the site as a county park since 1977. The swamp was designated a National Natural Landmark by the National Park Service in 1965.

Steep steps from the visitor center lead to the quarter- mile boardwalk that runs through the swamp. Bald cypress trees reach for the sky, while their knobby knees jut strangely above the water. With limited sunlight filtering through the dense 100-foot canopy of subtropical trees, the visitor might wonder whether he or she were really in Maryland and not hundreds of miles further south. Springtime brings a green carpet of skunk cabbage and ferns to the swamp, with pink accents from pink lady's slippers; swamp-loving cardinal flowers provide color in late summer. The sounds of spring peepers and green frogs and the chirping of songbirds add to the sensory paradise. Another trail goes through a hardwood forest. The nature center has exhibits on natural history, including a honeybee hive and native animals.

The boardwalk snakes around the swamp and allows views of the trees and plants as well as many animals, reptiles, and amphibians (including the snake pictured).

Calvert County

Above:
The cliffs composed of sand and clay contain one of the largest fossil-bearing deposits of exposed Miocene marine residue on the east coast of the continent.

Right:
Wetlands are home to amphibians and aquatic plants, and birds like to rest on the many dead trees.

The five-lined skink likes moist wooded habitats.

14. Calvert Cliffs State Park

Calvert Cliffs State Park is named for the twenty-four miles of Calvert Cliffs that project along the western shore of the Chesapeake Bay in Calvert County. The cliffs are famous for the fossils that fall from them and then are washed ashore to the nearby beach. The park offers thirteen miles of hiking trails on nearly 1,100 acres, hunting on an additional 550 acres, a one-acre fishing pond, a sandy beach for swimming, marshlands, fossil hunting, and a playground.

Southern Maryland was submerged by a warm shallow sea during the Miocene era 10 to 20 million years ago, and after the sea receded and the cliffs rose, the remains of prehistoric species such as sharks, whales, and seabirds were exposed in the cliffs. Sharks' teeth are commonly found in the waters off the beach, but over 600 species of fossils from that era have been found. A portion of the cliffs is directly north of the beach where swimming is allowed, but most of the cliffs and beach under them have been closed for safety reasons, due to cliff collapses.

The three and six-tenths of a mile round-trip Red Trail from the parking lot is fairly easy and goes through a diverse environment. After passing a quaint fishing pond with numerous sunning turtles, the trail and its bordering stream go through a shaded mixed hardwood forest. The stream then broadens into a large pond with wetland vegetation, finally draining into the bay near a beaver dam. Extensive views of the wetlands are seen from the trail before it ends at the sandy beach, cliffs, and the Chesapeake Bay.

The pond is at the entrance to the trailhead.

Serpentine brick walls enclose the formal boxwood garden, which overlooks the Sassafras River.

15. Mount Harmon Plantation

The nearly two-mile narrow entrance road lined with arching Osage orange trees will surely leave an enchanting impression on visitors to Mount Harmon Plantation, in Earleville on the Eastern Shore. Situated on a small peninsula and surrounded by water on three sides, the manor house sits on 200 acres of meadows, woods, ponds, and gardens. The property is most known for its preponderance of American lotus blooms in the bordering creeks. The house, one of the area's superb examples of eighteenth-century Tidewater plantations, is listed on the National Register of Historic Places. The property has been owned by the Friends of Mount Harmon since 1997, whose mission is to preserve and interpret the estate for the education and enjoyment of visitors.

The second Lord Baltimore, Caecilius Calvert, gave a land grant of 350 acres to Godfrey Harmon in 1651. Harmon built a tobacco plantation that flourished there for the next 200 years. The three-story, brick, Georgian-style house was constructed in 1730 on a small hill, bordered by McGill, Back, and Foreman creeks that empty into the Sassafras River. On early maps this area was called World's End. A Scotsman, James Louttit, bought the plantation in 1760, and in 1817, Sidney George Fisher became owner. Mrs. Harry Clark Boden IV, a direct descendant of those two earlier families, bought Mount Harmon in 1963 and furnished the house with English, American, Irish, and Scottish antiques from the period 1760–1810. She donated the house in 1974 to a national preservation organization.

The extensive grounds can be crisscrossed by trails that go through grassy meadows, through fields swarming with butterflies and bursting with wildflowers, along creeks filled with the American lotus and lined with rose mallow, on paths through woods of oak and flowering magnolias, and around magical ponds. A boxwood garden with a fountain and brick serpentine walls lends a formal air and is a great vantage point to view McGill Creek beyond, with its carpet of blooming American lotus in August. This plant is rare in Maryland and is a relative of the water lily. Close to the house are two 200-year-old English yew trees, an herb garden, and a tobacco garden. Outbuildings include a colonial kitchen and a tobacco prize house, used to compress tobacco for shipping. A pair of American bald eagles enjoys the property as well.

Mimosa trees in bloom overlook the lotuses in McGill Creek.

Zebra swallowtail butterflies are abundant in the meadows and grasses.

The tobacco garden plot is symbolic of the importance of the crop's role in the plantation's prosperity. The most northernmost prize house is located on the property; this is where tobacco was "prized" or compacted into barrels before shipping.

Near the prize house at Foreman Creek, a winding path through magnificent greenery leads to the pond. Dodder, the yellow stringy-looking plant, is parasitic.

Visitors will be mesmerized by the splendor of the lush woods, fields, ponds, and surrounding water.

Above:
The view from the back of the Mount Aventine manor house includes tulip poplar trees near the house and several types of oak trees in the sloping meadow to the Potomac River.

Right:
Large swaths of Eastern prickly pear cactus grow in the meadow. It is native to Maryland and is the only pervasive eastern cactus.

16. Chapman State Park

Cedar trees line the long entrance to the house.

Chapman State Park is one of the gems within the Maryland State Park system. It is part of a 2,254-acre property that was purchased by the state of Maryland in 1998 to save it from development. From the moment you drive up the cedar tree-lined driveway to when you look at the view from the back of the house down the sweeping meadows with mature trees to the Potomac River and Virginia on the other shore, you will be enchanted. Miles of trails will entice you, as you can walk among the meadows down to and along the Potomac River, in marshlands, or in the woods. The manor house, Mount Aventine, is one of the most important antebellum houses in Charles County. It was listed on the National Registry of Historic Places in 1996. The National Audubon Society designated the park an "Important Bird Area" for its many birds on the state's watch list. The Friends of Chapman State Park and Mount Aventine sponsor events throughout the year, including nature walks and programs.

Nathaniel Chapman, a wealthy Virginia planter, purchased the property in 1751 and his great-grandson built in 1840 a "side passage" house with a kitchen wing made from cut stone; it was enlarged twenty years later. The Chapmans were friends with members of George Washington's family and George Mason. The family businesses included a ferry boat from Chapman's Landing and later a fishery that lasted into the twentieth century. Its prominent location atop a hill made it ideal as a signal point for federal troops during the Civil War. Several owners occupied the house in the first half of the 1900s and in 1954, Margit Sigray Bessenyey, the daughter of an American heiress and Hungarian count, bought the property and other plots from the original tract. She bred and raised horses there until her death in 1987.

Many diverse environments make up the park. The spectacular walk through the meadow to the Potomac River goes past stands of magnificent old trees, many of which are different species of oaks. There are large patches of sun-drenched prickly pear cactus on the dry land. A short walk near the shore will take you to the family cemetery, and backtracking a small bit will take you to a path that goes through wetlands before starting the Marsh Trail. The Marsh Trail goes through a hardwood forest before it joins the large shrub swamp, with buttonbush and crimson-eyed rose mallow. Also included within the park is a rare shell-marl ravine forest with trees and plants more typical of mountainous regions. The park has a cherrybark, or pagoda oak, that is a state champion tree, and it recently lost an American basswood, a national champion tree.

Paw paw trees can be found on the Marsh Trail.

The great egret is busily hunting for lunch in the rich tidal marsh.

17. Blackwater National Wildlife Refuge

Blackwater National Wildlife Refuge occupies more than 28,000 acres of predominantly tidal marsh, freshwater wetlands, forests of mixed hardwoods and loblolly pine, and a small expanse of cropland south of Cambridge on the Eastern Shore. As part of the US Fish & Wildlife Service, it originated in 1933 as a refuge for migrating waterfowl. The refuge is one of the primary wintering grounds for Canada geese that use the Atlantic flyway, the East Coast's bird migration highway. Additionally, snow geese, tundra swans, and a variety of ducks can be found wintering on or migrating through the refuge.

The refuge can be visited by car or bike, or even a boat along the twenty miles of marked paddling trails. If you walk the third-mile paved path of the Marsh Edge Trail on the Wildlife Drive, many of your senses will be heightened as you smell the pines and the water, hear the grasses rustle, and feel the occasional light breeze accompanied by the sound of little ripples on the still water of the Little Blackwater River. The forest of tall loblolly pines and occasional oak give way to the marsh of mostly Olney's three-square bulrush, a flowering plant in the sedge family.

The Wildlife Drive, a six-and-a-half-mile loop road with many stopping points that goes along the marshes, ponds, and woods, allows ample opportunity to view the wildlife and the serene settings up close. Go to the observation site overlooking the Blackwater River and you will often see great blue herons and egrets searching for fish and shellfish, an occurrence common throughout the drive but always remarkable. Plants that can thrive in the marshes are tolerant of brackish water, and the list includes Olney's three-square, salt marsh bulrush, saltgrass, marsh hay, smooth cordgrass, and big cordgrass.

Two longer hiking trails through forests offer opportunities to spot mammals, amphibians, and birds. The Tubman Road Trail has a mixed forest of pines and hardwoods, and several wetland areas, hosting turkeys, frogs, toads, and the endangered Delmarva fox squirrel. The Key Wallace Trail has oak and beech trees, some of which are more than 100 years old. Owls, woodpeckers, and many other types of birds make their home year-round at the refuge. The refuge has one of the highest nesting densities of bald eagles on the East Coast north of Florida.

The wetlands are filled with many wildflowers, such as Queen Anne's lace.

The loblolly pine is somewhat tolerant of brackish water and periods of flooding. Many birds, including the bald eagle, use the trees for nest sites and perches.

The great egret has found a fish in the brackish water, filled with a cordgrass called *Spartina patens*.

Cordgrass, rose mallow, Olney's three-square, saltmarsh mallow, and Walter's millet grow in the marsh.

Frederick County

18. Cunningham Falls State Park

Located in the scenic Catoctin Mountains, Cunningham Falls State Park offers rugged mountain scenery, a recreational lake, and Maryland's greatest cascading waterfall, at seventy-eight feet. The park has two distinct parts, both with hiking trails: the lake, falls, and camping are located in the William Houck Area three miles west of Thurmont; while the historic Catoctin Iron Furnace, Scales and Tales Aviary, and more camping are three miles south of Thurmont in the Manor Area. In the 1930s, the federal government purchased land to create a recreation area, employing people through the Civilian Conservation Corps and the Works Progress Administration. The southern 5,000-acre tract became Cunningham Falls State Park and the northern tract became Catoctin Mountain Park, operated by the National Park Service.

The Catoctin Iron Furnace is listed on the National Historic Register and was the site of pig iron production from 1776 to 1803, making cannon balls for the Revolutionary War. Ruins of one of the three iron furnaces include a furnace stack and the iron master's Manor House.

The forty-four-acre Hunting Creek Lake has several sandy beaches, boat rentals, and opportunities for fishing; fishing is also allowed in the park streams. It is difficult to resist taking the short, easy half-mile Lower Trail from the lake to the falls. At the falls, you may again be tempted to climb the rocks to the top, or just admire them from below. Large rocks skirt the Lower Trail and informative trail signs state that the very old Catoctin Mountains were once the tallest mountains in the world; having been created from volcanic action, the rocks are some of the oldest rocks in the world. Although forests were widely logged to make charcoal to fuel the furnace, the park's extensive trail system goes through a dense mixed hardwood forest of tulip poplars, oaks, hickories, and maples. Some of the trails are strenuous to hike, but offer scenic mountain views.

Clockwise from top left:
The Lower Trail is an easy hike to the falls and it goes through a hardwood forest strewn with giant rocks.

Cunningham Falls Lake, also known as Hunting Creek Lake, features swimming, boating, and fishing.

Isabella is the second of three Catoctin Iron furnaces that were built, and the only remaining one. Trails lead from it to the park.

The War Correspondents Arch is a memorial to Civil War correspondents, as the practice of embedding journalists started during that war. The first tribute made in over 100 years after the memorial's construction was to honor four journalists who died in the post September 11, 2001, war on terrorism.

19. Gathland State Park

The mausoleum and burial plot built in 1895 are next to a scenic part of the Appalachian Trail.

Straddling both Frederick and Washington counties, Gathland State Park in Crampton's Gap was the site of fighting during the Battle of South Mountain, one of the first battles in Maryland during the Civil War. The War Correspondents Arch is the site's outstanding feature and was built to honor fallen war correspondents, the only national monument for them. The site is a national historic monument administered by the National Park Service.

The park was the mountain retreat of George Alfred Townsend (who added an "H" to the end of his initials to form his nickname Gath), who was the youngest correspondent of the Civil War. He later became a successful journalist, and bought the property for its proximity to Antietam and other Civil War sites. In 1885, he constructed an eleven-room house called Gapland Hall, followed by Gapland Lodge, servants' quarters. In 1896, the arch was built, standing fifty-eight feet high and forty feet wide. Its striking appearance is due to the rugged stone, a crenellated tower on the left side, three Roman arches atop a Moorish arch, niches with horse head carvings, and tablets inscribed with the names of 157 correspondents and artists of the Civil War. The park museum is housed in two of the buildings that have survived, and remains of the mausoleum and barn can also be viewed. In 1949, the Maryland Department of Forests and Parks acquired the property to make a state park, and the Appalachian Trail goes through the property.

The large stone barn in ruins has a plaque dated 1887.

Virginia bluebells are a springtime treat on the Ford Loop Trail that skirts the Monocacy River.

20. Monocacy National Battlefield

Monocacy National Battlefield is on 1,647 acres of bucolic farmland and forests in the Monocacy River valley just southeast of Frederick. It offers hiking trails through varying terrains with exquisite views of the serene countryside and historic farmhouses. In 1934, Congress established the Monocacy National Military Park to protect and conserve its historic, natural, and cultural resources.

Monocacy National Battlefield was the site of the third and final attempt by the Confederate Army to attack the North on July 9, 1864. The Confederate Army won the battle at Monocacy, but lost a critical day getting to Washington, DC, where Union troops were being reinforced. The fighting at Monocacy became known as "the battle that saved Washington, DC." The Visitor Center has excellent exhibits that show the advances of the two armies over the many farmsteads.

Several trails traverse the battlefield's natural areas, crossing fields and forests, and going along creeks and near historic houses. The Ford Loop Trail from Worthington House goes along the Monocacy River and in the spring, the Virginia bluebells are profuse among the lush green vegetation. Other spring blooms are spring beauty and yellow trout lily. Trees in this moist area near the river and Worthington's Ford, where Confederate cavalry crossed the river for their attack on the nearby farm fields, include such lowland trees as sycamore, paw paw, silver maple, and box elder. The trail continues along a peaceful cow pasture where Osage orange trees have been used as a living fence to keep in the livestock. The Brooks Hill Loop Trail can be added to the Ford Loop Trail and its steep ascent leads to a glorious view of the Thomas Farm. The Thomas Farm Trail or Middle Ford Ferry Loop Trail offer similar views. This is the same view that provided the vantage point to the Confederate General Jubal Early to gain victory. A few tagged white oak "witness" trees can be seen on this trail.

The Gambrill Mill Trail skirts a peaceful pond before the short boardwalk trail to the Monocacy River and the site of a former wooden bridge that the Union army burned under the direction of Major General Lew Wallace. More than 500 documented plant species have been found on the battlefield grounds, and several are state threatened or on the watch list, including dwarf larkspur and Short's rockcress.

The New Jersey Monument was the first of the five monuments established in the park. It was built and dedicated by the state of New Jersey to honor the services of the 14th New Jersey Regiment, which guarded Monocacy Junction.

The 274-acre Best Farm was purchased in 1993 by the National Park Service. Both Union and Confederate armies camped there throughout the Civil War.

Open cow pastures can be seen along trails at the Worthington Farm and Thomas Farm.

A Union field hospital was located near the pond at Gambrill Mill.

Sugarloaf Mountain sits high above the surrounding farmland and can be seen for miles around.

21. Sugarloaf Mountain

Sugarloaf Mountain is in Frederick County just north of Montgomery County, and it is a splendid reminder that that part of the state is still somewhat rural and even mountainous. And the views from the scenic vistas are awesome for a site so close to the large metropolitan areas of Washington, DC, and Baltimore. Sugarloaf Mountain has an elevation of just 1,282 feet, but it is more than 800 feet above the piedmont and rolling countryside southeast of Frederick. Because of its geological interest and beauty, the site is a Registered Natural Landmark.

Sugarloaf Mountain is privately owned and managed by Stronghold, Inc. Gordon and Louise Strong purchased tracts of land around Sugarloaf Mountain, and in 1946, a nonprofit corporation was established for the mountain property for the public's "enjoyment and education in an appreciation of natural beauty." Gordon Strong believed that "…those who appreciate natural beauty will be better people, people who will treat each other better." The mountain's name is derived from the shape of sugar loaves made during the days of pioneers. During the Civil War, the Union army used the summit as a signal station, and the log cabin at the foot of the mountain was a hospital for soldiers.

Sugarloaf Mountain is actually a monadnock, an isolated mountain that remains after the erosion of the surrounding land. It occupies approximately 3,000 acres and its cliffs on the summit are rugged and the trails can be challenging. There are about four trails of varying lengths that go through forests of oak, tulip poplar, black gum, and eastern hemlock, with seasonal wildflowers.

Scenic vistas to the east take in the rolling countryside of Montgomery and Frederick counties.

Washington Monument at the top of South Monument affords a glorious view of Cumberland Valley.

22. Washington Monument State Park

Washington Monument State Park is at the top of South Mountain near the border of Frederick and Washington counties. It offers spectacular views of the farmland 1,500 feet below, including the Hagerstown Valley and West Virginia. The park is named and known for the striking rugged stone monument, the first one that was built in memory of George Washington, a surveyor in western Maryland during his early years. The monument is maintained by the Maryland Park Service and was listed as a National Historic Monument in 1972.

On Independence Day in 1827, the residents of nearby Boonsboro erected part of the monument and completed it several months later. It fell apart several times in ensuing years and was used as a Union signal station. The Washington County Historical Society bought the monument in 1922 and deeded it to the state in 1934 for the development of the park. The current monument was rebuilt in 1936 by the Civilian Conservation Corps and stands thirty-four feet high. The tower is memorable not only for the panoramic views it affords, but also because it is shaped like a "milk bottle," made of rugged rocks.

Forty miles of the 2,000-mile Appalachian Trail go through Maryland, with the trail passing just below the monument. Mountain laurel provide colorful pink and white blooms in the forest during the spring. Many bird watchers come to the monument to spot hawks, eagles, and falcons, as the valley is a migratory bird flyway. Recreational uses include playing fields and picnic sites.

Picnic facilities and play fields are some of the recreational uses at the park.

The sundew plant is named for the gel at the end of its tentacles that gives it the appearance of having morning dew. The carnivorous plant eats insects that are caught in the sticky substance.

23. Cranesville Swamp

The 2,000-acre Cranesville Swamp is an astounding environment, full of rare plant, animal, and bird species. It is owned and managed by The Nature Conservancy, which first began to protect it in the 1960s. The property was one of the first National Natural Landmarks designated by the National Park Service in 1965, and it is one of the few boreal bogs surviving in the southern United States. Located near the western edge of the Appalachian Mountains, about half the preserve is in Maryland and the rest is in West Virginia.

Glaciers advanced toward Maryland during the last Ice Age 15,000 years ago, and after the climate warmed, many of the boreal plants survived. The swamp that was created is a boreal peat bog relic from the Pleistocene Epoch. This "frost pocket" that is situated in a mountain valley has cooler temperatures than surrounding areas and receives abundant precipitation. Peat results from compacted sphagnum moss, and the breakdown of the moss forms the bog, an acidic environment for other plants.

Five trails, each less than two miles, traverse the preserve. The 1,500-foot boardwalk crossing the swamp will delight the nature lover, as some of the forty-eight rare plants and animals in the preserve can readily be seen here. Each season brings its own appeal, as wildflowers appear in the spring, pink lady's slippers in late spring, and cranberries in the fall. The rare tamarack, or eastern larch tree, is a conifer that loses its needles in the winter, and it is visible from the boardwalk. It is a thrill to peer into the sphagnum moss surrounding the boardwalk and see the small carnivorous plants called the sundew and the larger pitcher plant. Cranberry plants and skunk cabbage are also found alongside the boardwalk. Further in the swamp rhododendron and mountain laurel are easily viewed. A logging locomotive went through the wetlands in the 1880s, leaving some small areas of virgin forest. Many other rare species make the swamp their home, including the small northern saw-whet owl, the rare Nashville warbler, sedge, and the endangered creeping snowberry, hidden deep in the bog.

Skunk cabbage and rare grasses and sedges are found in the bog.

The orange plant is haircap moss or *Polytrichum*, whose orange sporophytes stand up well above the leaves.

The southernmost natural standing group of eastern larch, or tamarack trees, is in the preserve.

LIFEGUARD ON DUTY

RESCUE

NO PETS

Mature trees provide shade near the sandy beach.

24. Deep Creek Lake State Park

Situated 2,500 feet high in the Allegheny Mountains in Maryland's panhandle, Deep Creek Lake State Park offers year-round recreational activities. The 3,900-acre lake is Maryland's largest and has sixty-five miles of shoreline, including many secluded coves. Although some parts are developed, the abundant views of pristine green forests and meadows plunging into the lake, with its colorful boats, are reminiscent of the magnificent lake regions in Europe. Moreover, the nearby ski resort even has a thrilling European-style alpine slide called a mountain coaster that offers glimpses of the lake during its 350-foot vertical descent.

The lake was formed in 1925 from a hydroelectric project constructed by the Youghiogheny Hydroelectric Company on Deep Creek. During this time, the forests of hemlock, white pine, virgin red spruce, and yellow birch were starting to be demolished by intensive logging. Nearly all the park's hardwood forests have regenerated from the early stands of timber, and oaks and hickories now predominate. The historic Brant coal mine and home site are within the confines of the park.

More than ten miles of hiking trails traverse the park, and one trail goes to the top of 3,000-foot Meadow Mountain, which forms part of the Eastern Continental Divide. The Meadow Mountain Trail even includes a section of mountain wetlands. The park also allows mountain biking, cross country skiing, and snowmobiling. The park has more than one mile of shoreline, several beaches, numerous vistas and picnic areas offering attractive views of the lake and mountains, and boat ramps. A Discovery Center offers educational exhibits of the natural environment, including the history of the coal industry, and birds of prey, reptiles, and amphibians.

The lake and mountains offer year-round activities.

The meadows are filled with wildflowers such as devil's paintbrush, whose name comes from its brilliant orange color that blends to a yellow center.

25. Finzel Swamp

Finzel Swamp, owned and managed by The Nature Conservancy, is a 326-acre nature preserve with more than thirty rare and uncommon species. Eight tracts were added soon after the original 1970 tract. Similar to Cranesville Swamp further west in Garrett County, the preserve contains boreal species that have endured since the last Ice Age. Finzel Swamp, however, is a fen, which means that its water supply is from groundwater at springs and seeps, not rainwater.

The trail from the parking lot crosses the swamp over several wooden bridges, tempting you to search the dark waters for some of the rare and uncommon plants and wildlife. Meadows are abundant with wildflowers, such as devil's paintbrush. The trail continues around a lake, and to the north, a small group of rare American larch trees are still standing in the forested swamp. The preserve is home to many uncommon species of birds and butterflies, and in the early spring you may witness the migration of the spotted salamander to its breeding ponds.

The lake is reached from the trail that traverses the swamp.

el Swamp is considered a fen and not a bog since groundwater, not rain, is the water source.

The swamp is home to eastern snapping turtles, such as this baby.

The fifty-three-foot Muddy Creek Falls is Maryland's highest free-falling waterfall.

26. Swallow Falls State Park

Tolliver Falls are the smallest of the four falls with a calm shallow pool.

Within its 257 acres, Swallow Falls State Park has four waterfalls, including the highest one in Maryland, Muddy Creek Falls at fifty-three feet. The oldest stand of hemlock and white pine trees in the state is also here, some of which are more than 360 years old. Old growth forests are those that have not been logged or changed substantially by people since the 1700s. The park's name comes from the hundreds of cliff swallows that formerly nested in a rock pillar below the upper falls.

The park originated in 1906 with the gift of nearly 2,000 acres from Robert Garrett, a Baltimore investment banker and philanthropist, and his brother. This donation was the start of Maryland's state forest system.

The one-and-a-half-mile hike through the forest takes you past all four waterfalls. If you go left upon entering, you will view Muddy Creek Falls, which has a lookout on top and below the falls. Its origin is in Cranesville Swamp in West Virginia, but it merges with the Youghiogheny River in the park. The path through the park passes large and interesting rock formations, as well as tall trees, rhododendron, and fallen trees from storms. Unfortunately, the park lost nearly half its trees from Hurricane Sandy in 2012. The next waterfall is Lower Swallow Falls, which is low and wide. Upper Falls has near it an impressive large rock with plants growing on it. And the last one, Tolliver Falls, is very scenic with its gentle falls and small water pool. Admission to Swallow Falls State Park allows one to enter the nearby Herrington State Park, which has a fifty-three-acre lake for swimming and boating; a five-and-a-half-mile hike through the Garrett State Forest connects the two parks.

The name Swallow Falls comes from the hundreds of nesting cliff swallows that used to make their home on the large rock.

Fox hunting was a hobby of Harvey Ladew, the creator of Ladew Topiary Gardens. The famous topiary includes the horse and rider, hounds, and fox.

27. Ladew Topiary Gardens

Ladew Topiary Gardens in Maryland's hunt country north of Baltimore has been acclaimed "the most outstanding topiary garden in America" by the Garden Club of America. It was also named one of the top five gardens in North America by the Canadian Tourism Council and was listed among the top ten most interesting public topiary gardens in the world by *Architectural Digest*. Both the house and gardens are listed on the National Register of Historic Places. In 1971, the gardens and house opened to the public, and the nonprofit organization Ladew Topiary Gardens, Inc., administers them.

The gardens are named after Harvey S. Ladew, who came from a prominent New York family that traveled extensively in Europe. He loved fox hunting and bought the 250-acre Pleasant Valley Farm in 1929 so that he could easily pursue his hobby in the open countryside. It was while he was fox hunting in England in 1920 that he first saw a topiary of a fox hunt, replete with fox and hounds. Not only did he recreate the fox hunt topiary but he added the horse and rider. After additions were made to the 1747 farmhouse, Ladew worked with local farmers to transform twenty-two acres into gardens featuring the remarkable topiary. His many trips to gardens in Italy and England had

Pine trees frame the Chinese junk topiary at the bottom of the Iris Garden. Large koi are in the pond.

instilled in him a love of long vistas and garden rooms, so he created them from two long axes and cross-axes. Although Ladew commissioned additional topiary frames after the initial hunt scene, he soon realized that he was capable of making them, and thus began his creation of many topiary forms. He was awarded the Distinguished Service Medal award from the Garden Club of America because of his skill in growing, training, and maintaining the topiaries himself.

The magic of the gardens begins upon entry as visitors are immediately rewarded with a view of the famed fox hunting topiary, made of clipped yew. The enchantment continues with fifteen garden rooms, beautiful vistas, and whimsical topiary. Garden rooms are based on a type of flower, such as the Rose Garden with hybrid musk and climbing roses, or a color, such as the Yellow Garden with yellow daffodils and golden privet hedges. The Terrace Garden near the house and the Great Bowl were the first areas Harvey Ladew worked on, shaping the hemlocks into topiaries of obelisks, swags, and four-foot-tall windows. Nearby, swans swim on wave-shaped yews that extend far down the lawn. Water plays a key role in many of the garden rooms. The Water Lily garden has pools with frogs and other aquatic life, and the Berry Garden with its fountain has plants full of colorful berries throughout the seasons. Large whimsical topiaries in the Sculpture Garden include seahorses, Winston Churchill's top hat, a victory sign, and a pierced heart. Summer concerts are held in the two-acre lawn called the Great Bowl.

The Terrace Garden has garlands, obelisks, and windows sculpted from hemlock trees.

Many large topiaries are in the Sculpture Garden. In the center is a pierced heart, a lyre bird is to the left, and a peacock to the right.

Nearly 100 types of irises are in the Iris Garden.

Cherubs welcome the visitor into the Berry Garden, where Harvey Ladew planted bushes with berries favored by birds.

The croquet court was formerly a tennis court. Seasonal plantings include irises and tulips.

Topiary swans sit atop wave-shaped yews that line one side of the Great Bowl.

Clockwise from top left:

The Brighton Dam is visible beyond the pink and red azaleas.

The garden is in a hardwood forest that is home to Maryland's state champion fringe tree.

The azaleas put on a showy display for several weeks around Mother's Day.

This new gazebo that was installed in 2012 offers a superb view of the Triadelphia Reservoir.

28. Brighton Dam Azalea Garden

Brighton Dam Azalea Garden is a five-acre garden with more than 22,000 azalea shrubs near Brighton Dam overlooking the Triadelphia Reservoir. With sweeping views of the reservoir and a backdrop of gentle forested slopes, the magnitude and brilliant colors of the azaleas make for a commanding scene. The garden is managed by the Washington Suburban Sanitary Commission, which manages the 800-acre reservoir. The idea for the garden originated with a former chairman of the commission in 1949, who wanted azaleas, dogwoods, and other flowering plants and trees to adorn the shoreline.

The plantings began in 1949 and the garden was established ten years later. Many of the early azaleas planted were of the Glenn Dale type, bred for their large flowers. Near the main entrance are several deciduous varieties, and these plants have flowers ranging in color from yellow- orange to orange-red. Several types of Kurune azaleas with early and late blooming flowers facilitate a longer season for the garden, but the general peak time is Mother's Day. A recently added gazebo was strategically placed so that one can view the scenic shoreline and the garden. Down a hill from the parking lot is an attractive picnic space with a play area for children.

The curious fawns appreciate the haven here.

The meadow's mountain mints produce many flowers that attract pollinating butterflies such as the Red Admiral.

The Audubon Naturalist Society, founded in 1897, is named in honor of John James Audubon, the ornithologist and naturalist who catalogued, painted and described the birds of North America.

Magenta flowers on the redbud trees at the bottom of the meadow signal spring.

29. Audubon Naturalist Society

The forty-acre Woodend Sanctuary in Chevy Chase is the headquarters of the Audubon Naturalist Society. Its mission is to inspire residents of the greater Washington, DC, region, through outdoor experiences, education, and advocacy, to appreciate, understand, and protect their natural environment.

John Russell Pope, the renowned architect, was commissioned in the 1920s to build the Georgian Revival estate on the eighty acres purchased by Captain Chester Wells, an American naval officer, and his wife, Marion Wells. Gardens planted by her have not survived, but many of the large ornamental trees have. The mansion is listed on the National Register of Historic Places and was bequeathed in 1967 to the Audubon Naturalist Society.

The property is an ideal place for families to explore, for the perimeter trail is less than one mile in length yet is rewarding in terms of wildlife observed. Deer are almost always seen year-round in the meadows or woods. The pond is especially inviting in spring when the bluebells abound near the edges and the tadpoles and frogs can be seen darting under the murky water. Two meadows pair off from the house and one can easily be immersed in the peaceful atmosphere of butterflies flitting among the wildflowers and birds fluttering around the bird feeders. Eastern hemlocks afford privacy around the site of the former tennis court that is now a popular setting for wedding ceremonies. Many native and nonnative trees are found throughout the property, some planted by the former owner and some grown naturally. Many native plants of the Chesapeake Bay Watershed are the focus of the Blair Native Plant Garden.

A magnificent view of Little Seneca Lake shows it framed in crown vetch, an attractive but aggressive invasive groundcover used for erosion control on hillsides.

Boaters and geese enjoy the pastoral beauty of Little Seneca Lake.

30. Black Hill Regional Park

The lake is popular with those who rent boats or have their own.

Black Hill Regional Park in Boyds is a 2,000-acre park with many hilly, wooded acres of oak, hickory, sycamore, and red maple, and its Little Seneca Lake occupies one quarter of the property. The park is managed by the Montgomery County Parks Department under The Maryland-National Capital Park and Planning Commission. The man-made lake was formed from the Cabin Branch, Little Seneca, and Ten Mile creeks, and the Washington Suburban Sanitary Commission owns the lake as a reservoir acting as an emergency water supply for the region.

Many miles of trails provide the hiker, biker, or horse-back rider with scenic views of forest, meadow, stream valley, and the lake. Because there is minimal residential development, most of the lake has beautiful unspoiled views of the woods. The shoreline is especially pretty in the summer as wildflowers such as rose mallow and New York ironweed add color. The Visitor Center has many nature programs for young and old that focus on the local ecology.

Boats are a fabulous way to explore the many coves and native wildflowers, such as the pink rose mallow and the purple New York ironweed on the shore.

The Choctaw crape myrtles have attractive smooth gray to cinnamon brown bark.
Japanese iris and other water-loving plants grow near the ponds and a nearby gazebo
provides a restful place to enjoy the scenery.

31. Brookside Gardens

Brookside Gardens is a fifty-four-acre public display garden within Wheaton Regional Park and administered by The Maryland-National Capital Park and Planning Commission. The gardens opened in 1969 with the mission to inspire people to garden by exhibiting easily accessible plants that grow well in the locality.

Various garden areas are defined by walls or shrubbery and visitors will most likely encounter newly blooming plants every time they visit. The Conservatories are at one end, featuring lush tropical foliage including tall banana trees and exotic bird-of-paradise plants. It becomes even more entrancing during the winter holidays with colorful poinsettias and a model train display. Warm months feature the longstanding *Wings of Fancy* butterfly exhibit.

Water is a prominent feature at the garden with two separate ponds in the Aquatic Garden and three interlinked ones in the Gude Garden. At the Aquatic Garden, irises along the ponds' banks and daffodils along the stream ensure a pleasant early springtime stroll. As the vibrant azaleas burst into bloom above the pond, another awesome walk is assured with nearly 2,000 azalea shrubs representing approximately 300 varieties. The ponds are full of life as well, with tadpoles, frogs, turtles, fish, and an occasional heron. The Anderson Pavilion, a gazebo overlooking the upper pond, is always a favorite of mine when the viburnum are in bloom because of the sensational fragrance combined with the early springtime views of flowers and water. The Gude Garden with the pond and Japanese Teahouse is a popular place for visitors, and the nearby turtles, koi, and geese are enthralling to watch. Large rolling lawns with walks and specimen trees allow for added enjoyment.

The Rose Garden has approximately 100 different cultivars of roses blooming from June through September. The nearby Trial Garden is a major attraction with 15,000 to 16,000 flowering bulbs in the spring. Later in the season, the garden becomes a theme garden or a display of unusual plants, and in the fall, a chrysanthemum garden, continually enhancing the understanding and enjoyment of the many visitors.

Several distinct garden areas comprise the formal gardens. The Perennial Garden, close to the conservatory, includes many plants that have adapted to hot, humid summers and cold winters. Beds of roses and tree wisterias, sequential blooms of alliums and asters, and a central pool of ever-changing aquatic plants, such as tropical water lilies, provide year-round interest. The

Fragrance Garden displays plants that are fragrant at some point in their cycle, including many types of edible and medicinal herbs, such as basil, mint, and fennel. Clipped yew hedges form the Yew Garden, creating a garden room in which colorful annuals and tropical plants shine against the darker background. The Maple Terrace is a well-planned choreography of thousands of blooming spring bulbs, ending with a brilliant, fiery show of Japanese maple foliage.

Great herons like to fish in the Aquatic Garden.

River birch trees frame the tulips near the Rain Garden.

Wisteria and lilacs make a winning pair with their color and fragrance in the Fragrance Garden.

Over 10,000 spring-flowering bulbs, including tulips, are planted in the Trial Garden.

Azaleas are reflected in the waters of the Aquatic Garden.

Damask horse chestnuts on the lawn overlooking the Gude Garden have a beautiful display of springtime blossoms.

The Japanese-style Gude Garden has a pond, teahouse, and gently rolling lawns.

Montgomery County

Clockwise from top left:

Steps from the nature center lead to a meadow with a large sycamore tree and wildflowers such as New York ironweed, goldenrod, and milkweed.

The attractive playground near the nature center has animals carved from wooden logs. Gray goldenrod and the yellow flowers of St. John's wort provide seasonal color.

The stream near the meadow is a popular place to skip rocks and wade.

The common milkweed is an important plant because so many species of insects, such as monarch butterflies, depend on it for food. The fruit is a green pod that turns brown and then releases many seeds.

32. Cabin John Regional Park

Cabin John Regional Park is a 500-acre park nestled near a heavily developed area of Bethesda. However, once you cross the wooden bridge that leads to its Locust Grove Nature Center, you will have entered a very enchanting natural world. The regional park, operated by The Montgomery County Parks Department under the Maryland-National Capital Park and Planning Commission, includes several miles of trails, a miniature train, several playgrounds, athletic fields, and recreational facilities, including an ice skating rink and tennis courts.

The Locust Grove Nature Center is situated high on a hill, its observation deck including bird houses and a frog pond. Adjacent to it is a wonderful natural playground with many animals sculpted from wood logs. Best is the steep trail leading down from the deck to a magnificent large meadow filled with wildflowers, including goldenrod, milkweed, and New York ironweed, that attracts fluttering butterflies. A very large sycamore tree stands at one end of the meadow, and trees in the neighboring woods include oak, tulip, maple, and locust. Children like to wade or throw rocks in the nearby gentle stream. One of the park's trails used by both hikers and mountain bikers, the Cabin John Trail, runs along the Cabin John Creek and leads into the forest, where there are deer and fox. The park's longest trail at nearly nine hilly miles is the Cabin John Stream Valley Trail, and it goes from MacArthur Boulevard to almost the edge of the city limits of Rockville.

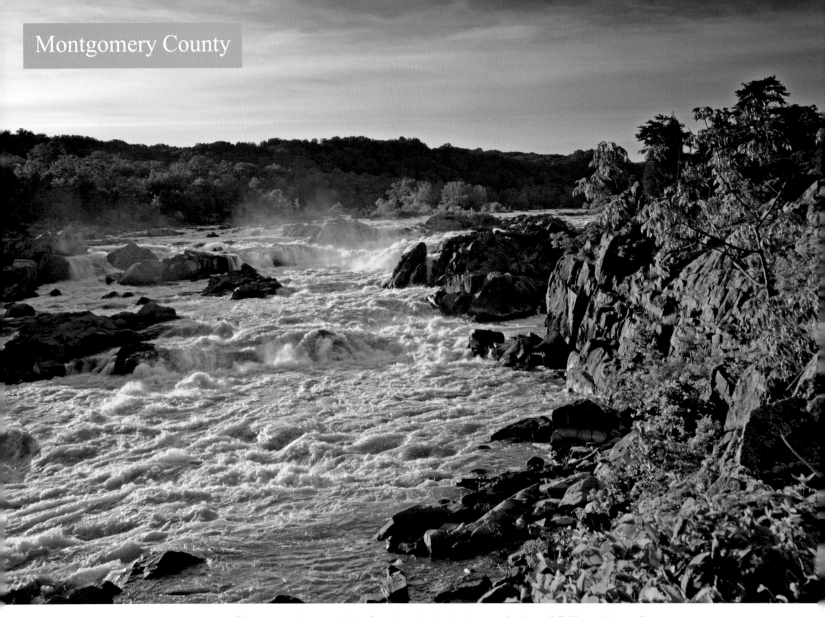

This view of the spectacular Great Falls is from the Maryland side, near the Great Falls Tavern Visitor Center.

This scenic stretch of the park is along Taylors Landing Road near Sharpsburg, and the Taylors Landing boat ramp has access for small boats.

33. Chesapeake & Ohio Canal National Historical Park

The Chesapeake & Ohio (C&O) Canal National Historic Park connects Georgetown in Washington, DC, with Cumberland, Maryland, spanning a distance of 184 miles and more than 19,000 acres. George Washington in 1754 envisioned a way to connect the eastern cities with the Ohio River Valley by building canals that would traverse the arduous parts of the Potomac River, such as the falls and rapids. The Patowmack Company began construction of canals in 1785, and their financial decline led to the rise of the C&O Company, which built the 185-mile canal on the Maryland side. A rise of 606 feet is managed by seventy-four lift locks, and other remaining C&O structures are the aqueducts, lock houses, and the Paw Paw Tunnel. The C&O Canal National Historical Park was established in 1971 by an act of Congress, ten years after it was declared a national monument. Five visitor centers are along its length.

Great Falls is the most well-known part of the park, as its dramatic cascades and rapids fall nearly eighty feet in a two-thirds of a mile stretch and are always a thrill to behold. The slow-moving river above the falls is almost 1,000 feet wide, but it turns into a torrent of rushing whitewater as it flows through narrow Mather Gorge, just sixty to 100 feet wide. An observation platform is at the Great Falls Park in McLean, Virginia, and near the Great Falls Tavern Visitor Center in Potomac, Maryland. Section A of the famous Billy Goat Trail is a one and seven-tenths of a mile hike through jagged wilderness involving rock scrambling but also offering breathtaking views of the Potomac River, Mather Gorge, rock pools, sandy beaches, and plants and animals. Great blue herons soar overhead in the gorge while colorful kayakers dare the currents.

Yellow prickly pear cactus grows near the rocks on the Billy Goat Trail.

The formal gardens on the eastern side of the house have many terraced levels created from steps and balustrades. Boxwoods border the rectangular lawn and daffodils provide spring color.

34. Glenview Mansion

Glenview Mansion with its formal manicured gardens is assuredly the showpiece of the 153-acre Rockville Civic Center Park. The estate was listed on the National Register of Historic Places for the significance of the architecture and gardens of the 1926 residence. The park's grounds include the Fitzgerald Theatre, the Croydon Creek Nature Center, and hiking trails, a playground, and tennis courts.

In the early 1700s, tobacco was grown and then replaced by grains such as corn, wheat, and barley; Muncaster Mill and Veirs Mill, located close by, were thriving grain mills in the early 1800s and an integral part of Rockville's economy. The Bowie family built a large farm and the core of the current house in 1838, naming it Glen View because of its valley views. They lived there until 1904. In 1917, Irene Smith purchased the estate. She married James Alexander Lyon, MD, in 1923, and together they made numerous additions. By 1926 they completed significant enlargements to the house to make it a neoclassical 25,000-square-foot house. The Lyons also created the formal gardens, pond, curved stone wall, bowling green, and a playhouse called the Cottage for their daughter. After the death of his wife, James Lyon sold the house in 1953 to the Montgomery County Historical Society and sold parcels of land to housing developers. The City of Rockville purchased the property in 1957 and bought additional acreage. The second floor of the Mansion now hosts art exhibits by regional artists.

The enchantment of the gardens at Glenview Mansion is highlighted by the discovery of many intimate garden spaces down the gently sloping hillside. The terraces formed by balustrades and steps, filled with old boxwood and vibrant yellow daffodils in spring, establish a look of formality and seclusion. A stone walkway runs the length of the garden, and arched entry stone gates at both ends afford an alluring portal to the secret gardens beyond. Several parterres are at the northeastern end of the formal garden: at the far end is a peony garden commemorating Rockville's growing friendship with Jiaxing, China. At the south end is a wrought-iron fenced garden with roses, boxwood, and a sundial, symbolizing Rockville's friendship with Pinneberg, Germany. Another small garden space with a fountain overlooks many acres comprising the glen. In the late summer pink blossoms on mature crape myrtle trees provide breathtaking color to the boxwoods surrounding the former bowling green. Beds on the front lawn provide seasonal color, and the cherry trees along the entrance drive create a magnificent welcome in spring. Originating at the Nature Center are hiking trails that cross the ever-winding Croydon Creek through the woodlands. A very large boulder overlooking the ravine affords an enjoyable view.

English boxwoods planted in the shape of a star are on the large front lawn.

Stone arches grace both ends of the stone walkway which is the garden's main corridor.

Cherry trees planted by the city of Rockville in the 1960s line the entrance drive to the Mansion.

Boxwoods enclose the former Bowling Green and to the left is the Cottage, or dollhouse. Old yew trees are located on the side of the Bowling Green near the Cottage and a large catalpa is on the other side.

The large catalpa tree, between the former Bowling Green and the field below, has beautiful large heart-shaped leaves and showy white flowers.

Montgomery County

McCrillis Gardens is spectacular in the spring with its azaleas and other flowering plants, such as the Chinese snowball viburnum on the right.

35. McCrillis Gardens

A springtime stroll in the five-acre shade garden in Bethesda is a ritual for those who come to delight in the garden overflowing with azaleas. Now managed by Brookside Gardens, the original owners William and Virginia McCrillis donated the garden to The Maryland-National Park and Planning Commission in 1978. William McCrillis had been a special assistant to the secretary of the interior for several presidents.

Winding paths go past hundreds of azalea shrubs, as well as many viburnum and rhododendrons in the spring. Trees, grasses, perennials, and annuals bestow color and texture throughout the year. The gazebo, many benches, and several lawns encourage one to linger and revel in the joys of nature.

A breathtaking springtime can be enjoyed from the gazebo.

The peak bloom time for azaleas is early April through June.

Bleeding hearts' common name comes from the fact that the flower is heart-shaped and it appears that there is a little drop of blood on the dangling part.

Pinxter azaleas are also known as wild azalea or honeysuckle, and they grow along stream banks or in upland woods.

The 'George Lindley Taber' azalea has showy variegated single petals.

White egrets and great blue herons are commonly seen in the marsh.

Paths in early fall are bursting with colorful wildflowers, such as goldenrod and purple-stemmed aster.

A jumble of yellow jewelweed, pink Pennsylvania smartweed, and light pink arrowleaf tearthumb is appealing.

36. McKee-Beshers Wildlife Management Area

Situated on 2,000 acres of woodlands, fields, swamps, and creeks near Hunting Quarter Road and the Potomac River in Poolesville is McKee-Beshers Wildlife Management Area. Reptiles, amphibians, and deer are often spotted on the many miles of trails, while the swamp attracts great herons, waterfowl, and egrets that can be seen wading on the distant shore. The Wildlife and Heritage Service of the Maryland Department of Natural Resources manages the land. Improving wildlife populations and their habitats while providing public recreational use of the state's wildlife reserves is the goal of the agency.

Many acres are planted with crops and grasses to feed different wildlife species throughout the year. Photographers and naturalists from far away are enticed in mid-summer by the sunflowers that seem to be endless. The tranquil wetlands are teeming with water lilies, or spatterdock, with their yellow flower balls and large green leaves, while along the shore, the hibiscus flower swamp mallow spreads with its white, pink, or red flowers. The hiking trails are flanked by many colorful wildflowers, such as goldenrod and pokeweed.

Fields of sunflowers are planted to attract game birds.

The young Eastern box turtle is enjoying a stroll at the management area.

The Pioneer Trail from Meadowside Nature Center leads down through a meadow to Study Pond.

The Pioneer Homestead near the Meadowside Nature Center is a historic site that includes the McClosky log cabin in the foreground, the Brown cabin in the background, the corn crib on the right, and also a smoke house.

The Valient Covered Bridge was built in memory of a local teacher and environmentalist.

37. Rock Creek Regional Park

Rock Creek Regional Park encompasses about 1,800 acres and offers a wide range of activities for people of all ages. It was probably the favorite park of my sons when they were young, as the gentle seventy-five-acre Lake Needwood is a good first lake on which to take young children rowing or pedal-boating, and the Meadowside Nature Center has many adventuresome and exploratory diversions. The park is managed by the Montgomery County Park Department, under The Maryland-National Capital Park and Planning Commission.

The Rock Creek Hiker Biker Trail runs about fourteen miles from Lake Needwood to the Washington, DC, border with Montgomery County, and can be extended further into the city via the bike trail along Beach Drive in Chevy Chase. Thirteen miles of trails traverse the park, passing through woodlands of oak, poplar, sycamore, and hickory, meadows, lakes, and ponds. If you take the Muncaster Mill Trail to the right of the Visitor Center and follow it along the North Branch of Rock Creek heading left, you will come across ruins of Muncaster Mill, a grist mill from 1820. Children will have ample opportunity to jump across the rocks in the stream or skip rocks. Another pleasant hike is Pioneer Trail; start from the Visitor Center and walk down through the meadow to Study Pond and beyond to the Pioneer Homestead, a historic site including two log cabins and other outbuildings.

Children adore the Nature Center because of the neat cave one can crawl through, which then allows a superb eye-level view of the turtles and fish in the pond. Also fascinating are: the room with snakes, toads, a box turtle, green frog, and insects; a room with old-fashioned toys and kitchen implements, an Indian canoe, and animal pelts; and the outdoor aviary with a barred owl, turkey vulture, and bald eagle. Lake Needwood offers both boat rentals and lake tours on its boat Queen Needwood. The park's other lake, the fifty-five-acre Lake Frank, boasts a three-and-a-quarter-mile Lakeside Trail, which provides delightful views of the lake and hilly woods to hikers and bikers. The park also includes an archery range, playgrounds, and a treetop adventure of obstacles including zip lines, swings, bridges, and trapezes.

The author's dog, Winston the English Setter, adores the view of the lake.

38. Seneca Creek State Park

Seneca Creek State Park encompasses 6,300 acres that include fifty miles of trails for hiking, mountain biking, and horseback riding, forests and fields for picnicking and hunting, a lake for boating and fishing, a formal peony garden, and several historical properties as well. The park's sixteen-and-a-half-mile Seneca Creek Greenway Trail goes from the park's northernmost point at Route 355 to its southernmost point at the Potomac River, near the Seneca Stone Cutting Mill ruins at the C&O Canal Towpath. The two main areas of this large park are the Clopper Lake area and the Schaeffer Farm Trail area.

The Clopper Lake area is the part of the park most known and used by visitors. Woods and fields border the ninety-acre scenic Clopper Lake, which offers seasonal boat rentals and fishing. Picnic tables are nestled in a dense forest of stately pine trees across from the playground and near the lake. There is also a mostly unknown wild five-acre peony garden with over 200 varieties that makes for a surprising and intoxicating visit in late May or June. The peonies were transplanted from the five-acre garden belonging to Washington, DC, realtor and avid gardener Edward Schwartz. In 1913 he started his world-famous five-acre peony garden with 250 varieties and 40,000 plants in Olde Town Gaithersburg. Now, the fifty by seventy-five foot formal peony garden at the park is in a field that once contained tens of thousands of flowers.

The Woodlands Trail near the park office is a very informative self-guided trail describing the life of Francis Clopper and his family, a tobacco merchant who built a twenty-one-room mansion in 1812 where the park office is located. The Cloppers planted many types of trees, and more than thirty are labeled and included in the Woodlands tree identification guide available at the park office. For example, there is a Kentucky coffeetree with its conspicuous stalked pods whose seeds were used as a coffee substitute during the Civil War. The log cabin situated at the site is the Grusendorf Log House, built in 1855 and moved from Germantown in 1994.

The Schaeffer Farm Trail section is a paradise for hikers, joggers, equestrians, and especially mountain bikers. Miles of trails meander along rolling hills and streams, and through forests and farm fields. Black Rock Mill, a former saw and grist mill, is a historic site on a scenic part of Great Seneca Creek in the Schaeffer Farm Trail section. It was built in 1815 and only its exterior stone walls remain. Another historic site is the Seneca Stonecutting Mill, whose ruins are in the woods off the towpath near Riley's Lock in Poolesville. This mill produced the rich red sandstone used in the construction of the Smithsonian Institution Castle and the C&O Canal. Just up River Road is the Seneca Schoolhouse, a one-room schoolhouse used from 1865 until 1910.

The Grusendorf Log House is one of the few remaining pre-Civil War structures in the Gaithersburg/Germantown area. It is surrounded by many different trees planted by the Clopper family who lived here starting in the early 1800s. The tree on the right is a maple tree.

Black Rock Mill is at a scenic point on the Seneca Greenway Trail and next to the Great Seneca Creek.

The Schwartz peony gardens consist of the display garden and five additional acres of peonies.

Spectacular views from Fort Washington include Washington, DC, upriver and Mount Vernon downriver.

The guard house is in the background, the officers' quarters to the right, and the flagpole and main parade ground are in the foreground.

39. Fort Washington Park

Situated on a hillside with commanding vistas of the Potomac River and Virginia, Fort Washington Park offers many historic and recreational opportunities. Its 341 acres consist of shoreline, meadows, and forests, allowing for hiking, biking, picnicking, birding, and fishing. The property is owned and managed by the National Park Service.

The first Fort Washington was completed in 1809 to defend the river approach to the nation's capital, and it was destroyed by its own garrison during the War of 1812. It remained the only defense for the capital until the Civil War, when additional forts were constructed around the city. In 1824 the existing stone fort was finished and large guns were later mounted. When the fort was downgraded to harbor defense before World War I, the large guns were removed. Transferred in 1946 to the Department of the Interior, the fort is one of the few remaining intact seacoast forts and the largest and only permanent masonry fort built before the Civil War to defend the capital.

There are about five miles of nature trails, including the River Trail that skirts the Potomac River near the lighthouse and then goes inland, and the Swann Creek Trail. The lighthouse, Light 80, was a fog bell tower initially and is now used as a channel marker for the US Coast Guard.

The thirty-two-foot tall fog bell tower lighthouse dates to 1882.

Small ponds in the nearby fields can be seen from the Visitor Center. It is a good place for viewing water birds such as herons.

Marshes along the Patuxent River are used by migrating birds.

40. Merkle Wildlife Sanctuary

Merkle Wildlife Sanctuary is the sole wildlife sanctuary managed by the Maryland Department of Natural Resources. Its 1,670 acres consist of hay fields grown for the 100 resident geese and the 5,000 geese that migrate there mid-October through March, the largest number of Canada geese on the western shore of the Chesapeake Bay. Edgar Merkle, a conservationist, spent much of his life providing for wildlife and succeeded in introducing Canada geese to his 400-acre farm in the early 1930s. The state bought his property and adjoining tracts to create the sanctuary.

The Critical Area Driving Tour connects the Patuxent River Park-Jug Bay Natural Area with the Merkle Wildlife Sanctuary, crossing over the Mattaponi Creek. On the trails and roadway across the tranquil property, you may often come across herds of whitetail deer, groundhogs scurrying across the fields of crops, or osprey and blue heron near the Patuxent River.

Four trails traverse the acreage, including the Paw Paw Trail, with its namesake trees and the largest fruit native to the state, and Poplar Springs Trail that shows off the sanctuary's champion yellow poplar, which is over 154 feet tall and more than fifteen feet in circumference. The picturesque view from the Visitor Center takes in some of the ponds and countless acres of fields.

Fields of hay are grown for the migrating geese and provide a nesting habitat for other birds. The road is part of the four-mile Chesapeake Bay Critical Area Driving Tour.

The colonial revival garden has beds of ornamental flowers, herbs, and boxwoods. Across the lawn is the summer house.

41. Montpelier Mansion

A span of parkland, 200-year-old boxwood, a colonial revival garden, and a one-of-a-kind triple blossom dogwood tree endow one of the finest examples of eighteenth-century Georgian architecture mansions in Maryland. The National Historic Landmark house is owned and operated by The Maryland-National Capital Park and Planning Commission (M-NCPPC).

The first owners, prominent Marylanders Major Thomas Snowden and his wife, Anne Ridgely, began construction of the house about 1781 on a high knoll overlooking the Patuxent River. It is a five-part Georgian country house with a central core and two wings and hyphens. Although only seventy acres remain now, it was a plantation on approximately 9,000 acres with outbuildings such as tobacco barns and slave quarters; their main business, however, was the mining and smelting of iron ore. Several notable guests such as George Washington visited Montpelier. It is said that he took boxwood snippets from the boxwood at Montpelier to grow at Mount Vernon. In 1961 the daughter of the last occupant, Ambassador Breckenridge Long, transferred ownership of the property to the M-NCPPC. The house is furnished with antiques and reproductions based on the estate inventory of the Snowdens' son Nicholas, who died in 1831.

The garden's outstanding feature is the charm and fascination of the fairly small colonial revival garden. From the parking lot, a meandering split rail fence, bordered with flowers, beckons the visitor to peer beyond and get a glimpse of the parkland with mature trees and the distant house. The brick path opens to a majestic view of the summer house, a rare hexagonal eighteenth-century garden house that is one of only two in the country that is on its original foundation. The summer house is a striking focal point at the end of the large lawn, with old boxwood hedges along the perimeter. In fact, the 200-year-old boxwood allée continues the length of the lawn to the house, even enclosing a maze. The unmistakable large tree between the house and garden is a 180-year-old Osage orange tree. If you visit mid- to late April, be sure to walk to the carriage entrance in the back of the house, where you will be dazzled by the triple blossom seventy-year-old dogwood tree; it is a one-of-a-kind tree with twelve petals per flower instead of the usual four. And lastly, the colonial revival garden enclosed in its little white picket fence with ornamental ball finials is magical. The green boxwood and white crushed oyster shell path provide a background for the colorful flowers and herbs to shine, and a sundial is in the center. Ornamental flowers are at one end, the middle section of herbs includes lavender, bee balm, and thyme, and the other end includes practical flowers, such as false indigo used for dying and roses used to make rosewater for use in baking. Large mature trees are throughout the property, including magnolias, horse chestnuts, and American sycamore.

A brick path with boxwood and hydrangea leads to the eighteenth-century summer house.

This one-of-a-kind dogwood has a "triple blossom" with twelve petals.

The garden at Montpelier Mansion includes a colonial revival garden, mature trees such as the large Osage orange, and abundant old boxwood.

The exquisite garden with pink peonies is enclosed by brick walls that impart an air of privacy.

42. Oxon Hill Manor

Oxon Hill Manor is a grand forty-nine-room Georgian style manor house perched on fifty-five acres that sweep down to the Potomac River. Located in Oxon Hill, just minutes from the Capital Beltway and National Harbor, the home is set in a serene parkland with beautiful formal gardens on the side and back. Oxon Hill Manor is operated by the Maryland-National Capital Park and Planning Commission (M-NCPPC) and was listed on the National Register of Historic Places in 1978.

The current property was part of a large parcel of land purchased in 1685 by John Addison. In 1710 his son Thomas erected a house close to the manor, and then his grandson Thomas Addison surveyed 3,663 acres and named it Oxon Hill Manor; when the latter Thomas died, his widow married the nephew of John Hanson, the first president elected by the Continental Congress under the Articles of Confederation.

In 1927, Sumner Welles and his wife, Mathilde, bought 245 acres and hired the famous architect Count Henri de Sibour to build the two-story home designed as an English manor house. Sumner Welles was the under secretary of state to President Franklin Roosevelt, who was known to have visited the property. Sumner and his wife hosted many diplomatic parties there. Sumner had an abiding interest in landscape design, had studied it briefly, and was able to apply his studies of classical landscape architecture to his property.

In 1952, Fred Maloof, an art dealer, purchased fifty-five acres and the manor to serve as a museum for fine art and John Hanson memorabilia. In 1976, the M-NCPPC purchased the property.

The parkland setting in front of the house consists of a large lawn with many mature trees. Behind the house with its large patio are acres of sweeping lawns with a view to the Potomac River in the background; it is a popular location for weddings and other events. On one far side, down a small hillside, small rose bushes surround an imposing reflecting pool with fountains. Close to the house are several formal garden areas, all with divine statuary, terraces, and attractive colonial-style brick walls. Niches for statues add to the enchantment. Low-lying boxwood and pansies provide shape and color to the formal gardens, and fragrant and colorful peonies add to the splendor.

The formal garden overlooking the Potomac River has statuary and a parterre filled with peonies and pansies.

Steps from the house lead to the reflecting pool, which is bordered by small rose bushes.

Sweeping views of the Potomac
River are beyond the formal garden.

The formal garden near the side front lawn
has terraces, statuary in niches, and pansies,
all surrounded by low brick walls.

Redbud trees herald spring at the Refuge.

43. Patuxent Research Refuge

Lake Allen at the North Tract of Patuxent Research Refuge is popular for fishing.

The Patuxent Research Refuge encompasses nearly 13,000 acres of forests, wetlands, and meadows and is one of the largest forested areas in the mid-Atlantic region, providing habitat for many migratory birds. The Refuge is one of more than 560 refuges in the National Wildlife Refuge System, which is administered by the US Fish and Wildlife Service. In 1936 the Refuge was established by President Franklin D. Roosevelt as the nation's only refuge to support wildlife research. The National Wildlife Refuge System is the world's largest group of lands and waters whose mission is to protect and conserve fish, wildlife, and plants, and their habitat.

The Patuxent Research Refuge is comprised of three tracts. The South Tract has the National Wildlife Visitor Center, five miles of hiking trails, and Cash Lake. Activities offered are seasonal fishing and tram tours, and the Visitor Center has interactive exhibits aimed at global environmental issues, endangered species, and migratory bird studies. The North Tract, the largest with its 8,100 acres and twenty miles of trails, offers hiking, biking, and fishing in seven locations. The Central Tract, closed to the public, includes offices and the Patuxent Wildlife Research Center.

The Refuge is home to some very old trees, including some former state champion trees that are now deceased. Popular trails near the Visitor Center include the Goose Pond Trail, which goes through a forested wetland area; the Valley Trail, going through an oak and beech hardwood forest; the Cash Lake Trail, taking in a transitional forest, of pine, beech, and hardwoods; and the Laurel Trail, with its abundance of mountain laurels. Be sure to see the show of Virginia bluebells and Jack-in-the-pulpits in the spring on the Little Patuxent River Trail at the North Tract.

The trail around Cash Lake goes through a hardwood forest of beech, red oak, and pine.

Mountain laurel, with the white flowers on the right, are abundant along the boardwalk trail that traverses a tidal hardwood swamp. Adjacent to the laurel and growing in the water is an ash tree.

44. Patuxent River Park

Jug Bay Natural Area is the headquarters for the Patuxent River Park properties, comprising 2,000 acres of land bordering the Patuxent River. Jug Bay is situated where the Patuxent River swells just north of the intersection of Prince George's, Calvert, and Anne Arundel counties. The longest river in the state, the Patuxent River flows 115 miles from the Piedmont region to the Chesapeake Bay southeast of Solomon's Island. The state in 1961 recognized the river as an important natural resource and subsequently The Maryland-National Capital Park and Planning Commission (M-NCPPC) purchased 8,000 acres of parkland to protect and preserve the river. The M-NCPPC and the Prince George's County Department of Parks and Recreation manage the park.

Since one of the largest tidal freshwater wetlands on the East Coast surrounds Jug Bay, it is one of the most important freshwater tidal estuaries in the Chesapeake Bay area. The National Audubon Society and the Maryland Department of Natural Resources have named it an "Important Birding Area" because of the unique species that live there, such as the least bittern and the sora rail. Hikers, bikers, and horseback riders can explore more than eight miles of woodland trails. The serenity of the water and wetlands is best appreciated by boat, either renting or bringing your own canoe or kayak. On the water, one can enjoy the turtles basking on the rocks, see the osprey nesting or flying overhead, and see and hear the large stands of wild rice swaying in the gentlest of breezes; the largest expanse in Maryland is here. The rice attracts many birds and waterfowl, and more than 250 species have been noted. The marshes are also home to large stretches of spatterdock, a type of water lily, and pickerelweed. In season, April to November, a pontoon boat tour is a great way to learn about the wetlands, wildlife, and history of the river. A four-mile roadway, the Chesapeake Bay Critical Area Driving Tour, connects the park with the adjacent Merkle Wildlife Sanctuary. Open to hikers and bikers most of the year and to vehicles on Sundays, it features a 1,000-foot-long wooden bridge across a marsh, an observation tower, and educational displays that prove why Maryland's Critical Area Act should provide special protections for land within 1,000 feet of tidal water.

The pontoon boat ride is a very pleasant and informative way to learn about the natural resources and history of the Patuxent River region.

The yellow water lily, or spatterdock, has large thick green leaves and yellow flowers and provides cover and food for many types of wildlife.

Osprey can often be seen in the nests at the Jug Bay Natural Area. A live webcam is pictured to the right of the nest.

Mrs. Calvert, the Mistress of Riversdale, loved to garden and had tulips sent from her father in Belgium. Even then, the many deer ate the tulips.

45. Riversdale House Museum

Riversdale House Museum, in the town of Riverdale Park, is a National Historic Landmark situated on eight acres of what was once a 2,000-acre estate. There is a pleasing garden on the front side lawn and the remaining acreage is lawn. The property is owned by The Maryland-National Capital Park and Planning Commission (M-NCPPC), and the Riversdale Historical Society, a volunteer organization, works with the commission to preserve the cultural heritage of the mansion.

Construction of the house was begun by Henri Stier, a Flemish aristocrat who fled Belgium with his family to escape the French Revolutionary Republic armies. In 1800 he purchased more than 700 acres near the port and spa town of Bladensburg and started building Riversdale in 1801. When the family returned to Antwerp after Napoleon Bonaparte offered an amnesty to émigrés, his youngest daughter, Rosalie, remained with her husband, George Calvert, a planter and descendant of the Lords of Baltimore. The federal-style house was completed in 1807, and it is a five-part, stucco-covered brick home with outstanding interior decorative details, including fifteen-foot ceilings on the first floor. For many years Riversdale housed sixty-three Old World paintings that Rosalie's parents had brought from Antwerp, including works by artists such as Peter Paul Rubens, Jan Breughel, and Anthony Van Dyck. A collection such as this in the United States was unheard of at that time. Rosalie Calvert was an avid gardener and in the salon she had four superb specimens of lemon trees. Rosalie and George had nine children, and one of their sons, Charles Benedict Calvert, was a farmer who was very interested in agriculture education and later founded the Maryland Agricultural College, now the University of Maryland, College Park. As a congressman, he promoted legislation to create a cabinet department of agriculture. The estate was sold in 1887 to develop the Riverdale Park suburb. Abraham Walter Lafferty, a former congressman and the last private owner of the house, sold the house to the M-NCPPC in the late 1940s. Restoration of the house began in 1988 and the house opened to the public five years later. The book *Mistress of Riversdale: The Plantation Letters of Rosalie Stier Calvert* provides significant insight into the lives of Rosalie and George Calvert, as well as America in the early 1800s.

Many of the vegetables, fruits, and flowers that Rosalie grew in the garden are still grown at Riversdale, including raspberries, fruit trees, roses, and tulips. Tobacco and corn were field crops in the 1800s and are grown in the garden now for demonstration purposes. Early spring brings many colorful tulips blooming in the large parterre in the side front lawn, an homage to the Stier family who sent tulip bulbs from Holland to their daughter. The compact size of the entire garden highlights the uniqueness and beauty of the plants. In summer the kitchen garden is glorious, as so many textures, colors, and sizes of foliage and flowers are competing for most distinguished-looking plant. One such majestic plant is the cardoon, or artichoke thistle, a tall plant with long slender leaves that appears to have a hat of purple flowers atop a crown of thistles. The light-green feathery fennel leaves contrast dramatically with the colorful, crinkly leaves of its neighbor, the Swiss chard. Planted nearby is scorzonera, an herb with long black edible roots that Rosalie requested of her sister in Europe. She also loved roses and decorative gardening, in vogue at the time, and the bright pink roses blend well with the muted pinks of the eye-catching, drooping love-lies-bleeding flowers. Off to the side is a large stand of pear, plum, cherry, and fig trees, a tribute to the orchard planted by the first owners.

Cardoons are a relative of the artichoke and grow into stately thistle-like plants.

The cotton blossom is a demonstration crop and is representative of the cotton used by Mrs. Calvert to make cloth for her servants.

In the side garden, the ornamental plant with the striking red, yellow, and green-tinged leaves is Joseph's coat, or *Amaranthus tricolor*, and the one beyond with the drooping pink flowers is love-lies-bleeding or *Amaranthus caudutus*.

The showy magenta flowers of the red bud tree on twigs, branches, and trunk become heart-shaped leaves.

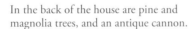
In the back of the house are pine and magnolia trees, and an antique cannon.

Gladiolus put on a show of color at Riversdale House Museum.

Frogs and turtles are easily spotted in the wetland.

The Children's Funshine Garden has many areas to explore, such as the sandlot, a bean teepee, and a sensory herb garden. The garden also contains a Three Sisters Garden that illustrates the idea of companion gardening whereby crops provide support for each other—in this case corn, squash, and beans.

46. Adkins Arboretum

Adkins Arboretum is the only public garden dedicated to promoting and preserving the native plants of the Mid-Atlantic Coastal Plain. Located in Ridgely on the Eastern Shore, its 400 acres within the 4,000-acre Tuckahoe State Park encompass a variety of habitats including meadows, forests, wetlands, and streams. The arboretum was named in honor of the Adkins family, staunch conservationists of the Eastern Shore and friends of the arboretum's first patron, Leon Andrus.

Enjoy the stroll over the bridge from the parking lot to the visitor center. It spans the splendid one-acre wetland and you will most likely spot turtles and frogs delighting in their environment. Five miles of intersecting paths go through dry open meadows, wooded bottomlands, and mature hardwood forests. More than 600 species of native trees, wildflowers, grasses, and shrubs are found in the arboretum. Trails skirt the large open fields filled with colorful grasses in the fall such as big bluestem and Indian grass with its soft golden plumes. Bordering the meadow edges are native wildflowers such as goldenrod, milkweed, and pokeweed with its clusters of purple berries. Other walks cross streams and pass stands of paw paw, poplar, and oak trees. Longer paths can be combined with the trails of the adjoining park, and biking and walking leashed dogs is allowed. Children will especially have fun at the arboretum, for there is a Paw Paw Playground with two wigwams and snake balance beam, a Children's Funshine Garden, and a small herd of goats to help manage non-native invasive plants.

Wildflowers, such as white-flowered pearly everlasting, and grasses, such as purple love grass and big bluestem, are found in the meadows.

The male Osage orange tree near the library's patio is "the champion tree of Washington College."
The bark is orange-brown and has lighter colors in the gnarled furrows.

47. The Washington College Virginia Gent Decker Arboretum

Washington College is a small four-year liberal arts college on 112 acres in Chestertown on the Eastern Shore, and in 1782 it was the first college chartered in the new country. George Washington gave the college a founding gift of fifty guineas and gave permission to use his name, and more recently, two holly trees from Mount Vernon have been given as a gift. The arboretum was established in 1996, and two years later was named in honor of Virginia Gent Decker, the wife of the retired chief executive officer of Black & Decker Corporation, due to her appreciation for the natural environment and support of the college.

Many colleges and universities have their own arboretum, or a place where many kinds of trees and shrubs, mostly labeled, are cultivated for scientific and educational purposes. The arboretum used Mount Vernon as its model and used existing trees and shrubs as the basic plantings. More than 700 trees representing over ninety species are on campus. Teaching, research, public education, recreation, and collections are the roles of the arboretum.

The beautiful landscaping and plantings enhance the attractiveness of the colonial-style campus of brick buildings. Even without many ornamental plants, the abundance of the large trees, with their various textures and colors of leaves and bark, provide a colorful setting for the peaceful grounds. River birch and London plane trees, boasting their glorious bark, line the walkways near some of the dormitory areas.

Large Japanese pagoda trees grace the front lawn of Daly Hall. Their white flowers bloom late in the summer, and the fruit is a cluster of green pods that turn yellow or brown in the fall.

The deodar cedar tree near the library is evergreen and a popular ornamental tree. Cones of the tree take two to three years to grow.

Two blue atlas cedar trees frame the front of Hodson Hall and in the foreground is a bust of George Washington and a crape myrtle tree.

Queen Anne's County

The Ferry Landing Trail has a canopy of Osage orange trees. The trees were used by Native Americans to make bows and were used by farmers to make hedgerows and fence posts.

Opposite, Clockwise from top left:
Drum Point is the scenic cove at the end of the Ferry Landing Trail.

Purpletop grass is in beds along the Holly Tree Trail.

The nearly 300-year-old holly tree is near borders of wildflowers, including tickseed sunflower and jewelweed.

A bucolic view is afforded by the wheat fields and barn.

48. Wye Island Natural Resources Management Area

Wye Island Natural Resources Management Area is a 2,450-acre preserve with a secluded atmosphere worth visiting in any season. The Maryland Department of Natural Resources manages nearly all of the island's 2,800 acres for agriculture, recreation, and resource management, and the fields and twelve miles of hiking trails through the property are unique and memorable for their serenity and beauty. South of Queenstown, the island is located between the Wye River and the Wye East River.

For more than 300 years, the island was privately owned and used for farming, primarily wheat and tobacco. William Paca and Charles Beale Bordley were two early famous owners, the latter ensuring the island's fortune through vineyards, orchards, a brewery, and textile production. The hunting lodge Duck House on Granary Creek was built by later owners Glenn and Jacqueline Steward, who had a cattle ranch on the island. The state of Maryland in the 1970s bought the island to safeguard its preservation when there was a risk of residential development. The main reason for the purchase was that the thirty miles of undisturbed shoreline provide a waterfowl winter resting area and migratory stopover.

The main road through forests and fields of soybeans, corn, and wheat that leads to the trails provides stunning vistas of the land, water, and wildlife. The Ferry Landing Trail goes under a magnificent aromatic canopy of twisted Osage orange trees and ends at a secluded sandy beach at Drum Point. The Holly Trail goes alongside lush fields of soybeans and grasses and beds of wildflowers and within a few moments the nearly 300-year-old holly tree is in view. The thirty-acre stand of mature oaks, black gum, and hickory seen on the Schoolhouse Woods Nature Trail is one of the largest old growth forest remnants on the Eastern Shore. Some of the trails interconnect and end at their own sheltered coves. Wildlife such as the endangered Delmarva fox squirrel may be seen while hiking; in addition, hikers and especially paddlers may see bald eagles and osprey in trees along the shore and mallards, ducks, egrets, and herons in the many coves.

At the Woodland Indian Hamlet, the covering for the long house, or witchott, is made of phragmites, a perennial grass found in wetlands. A yucca grows in front of the house and to the right are sunflowers.

49. Historic St. Mary's City

Historic St. Mary's City is the site of the former first capital of Maryland and the fourth permanent English settlement in North America. It is one of the country's best preserved colonial archaeological settings and was designated a National Historic Landmark in 1969. On approximately 800 acres, it is a living history museum with re-created buildings and garden areas amidst the forests and countryside.

King Charles I of England wanted to develop colonies in the New World that would foster trade with England and he gave a land grant to Cecil George Calvert, the second first Lord of Baltimore. The colony at St. Mary's City was established in 1634 by about 140 English settlers who claimed the land from the Yaocomaco Indians. The early colonists planted Indian corn for food and tobacco for trade. In 1695 the capital was moved to Annapolis. As a result, St. Mary's City was abandoned for hundreds of years. Interest in the site was revived in the early twentieth century, and archaeologists continue to work uncovering evidence of the past.

The different garden areas represent different time frames during the sixty years that St. Mary's City flourished. In all the outdoor exhibits, the costumed staff provide a very informative, fun learning experience about the former uses of the plants, especially those you can touch, smell, and even taste.

The Woodland Indian Hamlet is a replica of the settlement in which the early colonists lived with the Yaocomaco Indians. The long houses, or witchotts, are made of phragmites, a perennial grass found in the wetlands and used for thatching roofs. You can see the yucca plant growing and a demonstration of the strength of the cord made from its fibers. There is a Native American Three Sisters garden comprised of corn, beans, and squash that is an example of an early sustainable companion garden in which the three vegetables are planted in close proximity. The corn stalks enable the bean vines to rise, the beans improve the soil's fertility, and the squash acts as a mulch to prevent weeds and other predators from attacking the vegetables. Most importantly, the three vegetables provide a balanced diet.

The Town Center includes Smith's Ordinary, a re-created inn from the late 1600s, and several garden beds with vegetables and herbs used for cooking, medicinal, and other purposes. Painted lady beans and scarlet runner beans with beautiful ornamental scarlet and white bi-color, and red flowers, respectively, grow enthusiastically up the teepee trellis and were commonly planted by early colonists. The knowledgeable staff will explain the many uses of tansy, the plant with the yellow button-like flowers, including as flavoring for omelets and puddings, as a dye, and as a remedy for bloating. Nearby one can smell rue and see why colonists thought it protected them from evil spirits and plagues.

Costumed staff in the larger Godiah Spray Plantation Garden will educate you on the vegetables and herbs used for cooking, medicinal, and other purposes. Horsetail grass, or equisetum, is planted along the entrance of the garden, and as you touch the abrasive stems, you will see why it was used to scour pots or mugs. Monarda, or bee balm, with its attractive red flowers had medicinal benefits, including its use as an antiseptic. The many fruit trees include fig trees, dwarf pear, and medlar, similar to an apple tree but used to make jelly.

Fennel, tansy with its yellow button-like flowers in the center, and rue are some of the plants grown at Smith's Ordinary at Town Center.

Tobacco is grown in one of the fields at the recreated 1660s Godiah Spray Plantation.

Showy scarlet runner beans make fast-growing beautiful vines.

Red poppies and purple irises make a colorful framework for the sweeping lawn and the Patuxent River beyond.

50. Sotterley Plantation

Overlooking the Patuxent River on ninety-five acres of rolling meadows, gardens, and shoreline sits the stately Sotterley Plantation. It is the only surviving Tidewater plantation in Maryland open to the public. It is comprised of the main plantation house built in 1703, approximately twenty outbuildings including a slave cabin from the 1830s, trails, and the magnificent gardens. The property is governed by a board of trustees, which includes descendants of former owners and slaves. The gardens are maintained by the Sotterley Garden Guild, a group of volunteers.

James Bowles, a tobacco and lumber trader, and the son of a prosperous London businessman, purchased 2,000 acres near the Patuxent River in 1699. Four years later he had completed the two-room plantation house using post-in-ground construction. When he died, his wife married George Plater II, and it was their son, George Plater III, who named the plantation Sotterley, after the Platers' family home in Sussex, England. As the plantation grew to about 7,000 acres, the number of slaves increased to more than ninety. During the Revolutionary War, the War of 1812, and the Civil War, many of the slaves escaped to fight for the North. The property exchanged hands several times until the early 1900s when Herbert Satterlee and his wife, Louisa Pierpont Morgan Satterlee, the daughter of J. P. Morgan, bought the 1,000-acre Sotterley plantation. They constructed the colonial revival garden and used their vision to re-create the eighteenth-century plantation. Their daughter Mabel Satterlee Ingalls bought the estate in 1947 and also enjoyed working in the garden. In 1961 she created a nonprofit historic foundation and opened the plantation house for tours, and in 2000 it was named a National Historic Landmark.

The gardens were first designed in the early and mid -1900s, when the Satterlees divided the land into geometric plots and planted perennial beds, an herb garden, a vegetable plot, and a cutting garden. Looking beyond the long peony border and the necessary, or outhouse, to a view of the Patuxent River is just one of the enchanting views at Sotterley. Walking toward the plantation house, there is an even more awe-inspiring vista down the lawns toward the Patuxent, taking in the poppies in late spring or the purple phlox and orange lilies in mid-summer. The scene is very peaceful, especially in the late afternoon when the butterflies and bees hover, and the colors and textures form an exquisite view. The last garden bed before the rolling meadow includes dahlias, lacecap hydrangea, and a fragrant blush noisette rose near the plantation house, which may have been planted by the Satterlees. The cistern was brought by the Satterlees, and the restored sundial is thought to date from the late nineteenth century. A small children's garden was planted near the necessary and now has several miniature trees more than twenty years old, including a redbud, sweetgum, and hornbeam. Overall, the rows of flowers have been planted with such attentiveness to the colors and masses of flowers that enhance the vistas in every direction, creating a paradise of flowers.

The herb garden is divided into separate plots including medicinal, aromatic, and culinary plants, and many are labeled. Some of the medicinal plants are black-eyed Susans, comfrey, and a blackberry lily with a pretty orange flower with pink dots; some of the aromatic plants are a red monarda and sweet annie, and the culinary ones include sage and an unusual-looking Egyptian walking onion, or tree onion. A dedicated group of volunteers tends the gardens to create the masterpiece here.

The gardens are known for the long row of peonies along the brick wall.

The formal garden has yew topiary and a restored nineteenth-century sundial. Purple phlox in the background frame the Patuxent River.

The delicate cosmos flowers with their airy feathery leaves flutter in the lightest breezes. Gladiolus are in the foreground and crape myrtle trees bloom in the background.

The culinary herb garden includes plants such as basil, rosemary, and Egyptian walking onions. The plantation house is in the background.

Phlox and lilies provide seasonal color to a beautiful view of the Patuxent River.

The monument to the 130th Pennsylvania Volunteers Infantry stands vigil over a curvy stretch of the Sunken Road. In the foreground is the monument to the 8th Ohio Infantry Regiment.

51. Antietam National Battlefield

Antietam National Battlefield in Sharpsburg is comprised of 3,263 acres of farmland, forests, and pastures. It is the site of the bloodiest one-day battle in American history; 23,000 soldiers died or went missing on September 17, 1862, during twelve hours of fighting. Since the Confederate Army of Northern Virginia failed in its mission and it was the first major Civil War battle on Northern territory, the outcome gave President Lincoln the confidence to issue the Emancipation Proclamation. The battlefield and cemetery were established by Congress in 1890 and transferred to the National Park Service in 1933.

Antietam is a well-preserved battlefield, containing ninety-six monuments, more than 500 cannons, and many historic snake, worm, or zigzag fences. One of the most historic and symbolic structures is Burnside Bridge, which is near the largest wooded area called Snavely Woods. An observation tower at one end of Sunken Lane offers impressive views of the countryside and also provides the visitor with a better understanding of the battle action. In the near distance the Mumma and Roulette farmsteads, which existed during the war, can be seen. The Sunken Road was later called Bloody Lane because of the intense fighting that occurred there.

The countryside is beautiful, and there are numerous vistas of pastureland and monuments, with gentle, solemn mountains in the background. The stunning scenery contrasts with the horrific events of the past. As you walk the grounds, the eerie silence is broken by the gentle breezes rustling the corn stalks and soybeans. Environmental restoration projects are ongoing, and autumn meadows filled with wildflowers such as goldenrod and asters are a testament to that success.

Burnside Bridge, named after Major General Ambrose Burnside, is where roughly 500 Confederates tried to prevent 12,000 Union troops from crossing in a three-hour battle. The American sycamore tree at the north end of the bridge is about 170 years old and is a witness tree.

The bucolic scenery belies the fact that fighting at nearby South Mountain occurred just three days prior to the battle at Antietam.

Fields of corn and soybeans surround Mumma's Farm, the only civilian structure intentionally set on fire during the battle. It was rebuilt immediately following the battle.

The Final Attack Trail goes through scenic countryside, but it was the site of two and half hours of fighting, concluding the bloodiest day of battle in American history.

Ever-changing displays of flowers greet visitors at the Visitor Center.

Wild horses roam the dunes to eat beachgrass and saltmarsh cordgrass in the marshes. Courtesy of Meghan Sochowski.

52. Assateague State Park

Assateague State Park is Maryland's only state park right on the ocean, and it is also known for its herd of approximately 100 wild horses. The park is on Assateague Island, a thirty-seven-mile long barrier island between the Atlantic Ocean and Sinepuxent Bay, of which the northern two-thirds of the island are in Maryland and the southern third is in Virginia. Two miles of wide undeveloped beaches allow for swimming and fishing, the bay side has coves to explore for kayakers and canoeists, and opportunities abound for all to observe the wild horses grazing on the dunes or in the marsh, running on the beaches, or posing for photos.

Located on the Atlantic flyway, more than 200 species of birds, including herons, eagles, and ducks, have been observed. In the ocean, dolphins can be seen frolicking and fishermen are likely to find rockfish and trout. Horseshoe crabs and white-spotted silka deer are other wildlife commonly seen. Half a mile from the Visitor Center, which houses a nature center, is Rackliffe House, a restored eighteenth-century coastal plantation house overlooking Sinepuxent Bay; it is the only one of its kind open to the public in the mid-Atlantic area.

Many types of plants thrive in the different coastal environments at the park. Although the sand dunes are subject to salt spray and constant heat, American beachgrass flourishes and is a source of food for the horses, while also stabilizing the dunes with its horizontal runners. Wildflowers play dual roles as well, and they can be found in all the different island environments. Seaside goldenrod blankets the dunes in late summer while white-flowered rose mallow and white, purple, and pink flowered asters grow near the roads.

Migrating monarch butterflies feast on the fall-blooming seaside goldenrod. Courtesy of Meghan Sochowski.

Wild horses on the beach are an exhilarating sight. Courtesy of Meghan Sochowski.

Allegheny County

Rocky Gap State Park
12500 Pleasant Valley Road NE, Flintstone, MD 21530
(301) 722-1480
www.dnr.state.md.us/publiclands/western/rockygap.asp
Open 7 AM–dusk; $

Anne Arundel County

Helen Avalynne Tawes Garden
580 Taylor Avenue, Annapolis, MD 21403
(410) 260-8189
www.dnr.state.md.us/publiclands/tawesgarden.asp
Open dawn to dusk; free

Historic London Town and Gardens
839 Londontown Road, Edgewater, MD 21307
(410) 222-1919
www.historiclondontown.org
Open Wed.–Sat., 10 AM–4:30 PM; Sun., 12–4:30 PM; $

William Paca House and Garden
186 Prince George Street, Annapolis, MD 21401
(410) 990-4543
www.annapolis.org
Open Mon.–Sat., 10 AM–5 PM, Sun., 12–5 PM; $

Baltimore City

Baltimore Museum of Art Sculpture Garden
10 Art Museum Drive, Baltimore, MD 21218
(443) 573-1700
www.artbma.org
Open Wed.–Fri., 10 AM–dusk, Sat.–Sun., 11 AM–dusk; free

Cylburn Arboretum
4915 Greenspring Avenue, Baltimore, MD 21209
(410) 367-2217
www.cylburn.org
Open Tues.–Sun., 8 AM–5 PM; free

Evergreen Museum & Library
4545 N. Charles Street, Baltimore, MD 21210
(410) 516-0341
www.museums.jhu.edu/evergreen.php
Open Tues.–Fri., 11 AM–4 PM, Sat.–Sun., 12–4 PM; gardens
open until 4:30; $

Fort McHenry National Monument and Historic Shrine
2400 East Fork Avenue, Baltimore, MD 21230
(410) 962-4290
www.nps.gov/fomc
Open 9 AM–5 PM regular hours; $

Howard Peters Rawlings Conservatory & Botanic Gardens

3100 Swan Drive, Baltimore, MD 21217

(410) 396-0008

www.rawlingsconservatory.org

Open Wed.–Sun., 10 AM–4 PM; free; donations

Sherwood Gardens

4100 Greenway, Baltimore, MD 21218

(410) 785-0444

www.guilfordassociation.org/sherwood

Open all hours; free

Baltimore County

Hampton National Historic Site

535 Hampton Lane, Towson, MD 21286

(410) 823-1309

www.nps.gov/hamp

Open Thur.–Sun., 10 AM–4 PM for house tours; garden open daily; free

Calvert County

Annmarie Sculpture Garden & Arts Center

13480 Dowell Road, Solomons, MD 20629

(410) 326-4640

www.annmariegarden.org

Open daily 9 AM–5 PM; $

Battle Creek Cypress Swamp

2880 Grays Road, Prince Frederick, MD 20678

(410) 535-5327

www.dnr.state.md.us/wildlife/publiclands/Natural_Areas/BattleCreek.asp

Open Mon.–Fri., 9 AM–4:30 PM; Sat., 10 AM–6 PM; Sun., 1 PM–6 PM; free

Calvert Cliffs State Park

9500 H. G. Trueman Road, Lusby, MD 20657

(301) 743-7613

www.dnr.state.md.us/publiclands/southern/calvertcliffs.asp

Open daily sunrise to sunset; $

Cecil County

Mount Harmon Plantation

600 Mount Harmon Road, Earleville, MD 21919

(410) 275-8819

www.mountharmon.org

Open May–October, Thur.–Sun., 10 AM–3 PM; $

Charles County

Chapman State Park

3452 Ferry Place, Indian Head, MD 20640

(301) 743-7613

www.dnr.state.md.us/publiclands/southern/chapman.asp

Open daily sunrise to sunset; free

Dorchester County

Blackwater National Wildlife Refuge

2145 Key Wallace Drive, Cambridge, MD 21613

(410) 228-2677

www.fws.gov/refuge/blackwater

Open dawn to dusk; $

Frederick County

Cunningham Falls State Park

14039 Catoctin Hollow Road, Thurmont, MD 21788

(301) 271-3676

www.dnr.state.md.us/publiclands/western/cunningham.asp

Open 8 AM–sunset; $

Gathland State Park
900 Arnoldstown Road, Jefferson, MD 21755
(301) 791-4767
www.dnr.state.md.us/publiclands/western/gathland.asp
Open sunrise to sunset; free

Monocacy National Battlefield
5201 Urbana Pike, Frederick, MD 21704
(301) 662-3515
www.nps.gov/mono
Visitor Center open daily 8:30 AM–5 PM; free

Sugarloaf Mountain
7901 Comus Road, Dickerson, MD 20842
(301) 869-7846
www.sugarloafmd.com
Open sunrise to sunset; free

Washington Monument State Park
6620 Zittlestown Road, Middletown, MD 21658
(301) 791-4767
www.dnr.state.md.us/publiclands/western/washington.asp
Open Apr.–Oct., 8 AM–sunset; Nov.–Mar., 10 AM–sunset; $

Garrett County

Cranesville Swamp Nature Preserve
Lake Ford Road, Oakland, MD
(301) 897-8570 (The Nature Conservancy)
www.dnr.state.md.us/wildlife/publiclands/natural_areas/
Cranesville_Swamp.asp
Open dawn to dusk; free

Deep Creek Lake State Park
808 State Park Road, Swanton, MD 21561
(301) 387-5563
www.dnr.state.md.us/publiclands/western/deepcreek.asp
Open daily 8 AM–sunset; $

Finzel Swamp
Cranberry Swamp Road, Finzel, MD 21532
(301) 897-8570 (The Nature Conservancy)
www.dnr.state.md.us/wildlife/publiclands/natural_areas/Finzel_
Swamp.asp
Open year-round, daylight hours; free

Swallow Falls State Park
222 Herrington Lane, Oakland, MD 21550
(301) 387-6938
www.dnr.state.md.us/publiclands/western/swallowfalls.asp
Open March–Oct., 8 AM–sunset; Nov.–Feb.,m 10 AM–sunset; $

Harford County

Ladew Topiary Gardens
3535 Jarrettsville Pike, Monkton, MD 21111
(410) 557-9570
www.ladewgardens.com
Open April 1–Oct. 31, weekdays 10 AM–4 PM; weekends 10
AM–5 PM; $

Howard County

Brighton Dam Azalea Garden
2 Brighton Dam Road, Brookeville, MD 20833
(301) 206-8233
www.gardenvisit.com/garden/brighton_dam_azalea_garden
Open daily during blooming season, 9 AM–7 PM; free

Montgomery County

Audubon Naturalist Society
8940 Jones Mill Road, Chevy Chase, MD 20815
(301) 652-9188
www.audubonnaturalist.org
Open dusk to dawn; free

Black Hill Regional Park
20930 Lake Ridge Drive, Boyds, MD 20841
(301) 528-3490
www.montgomeryparks.org/facilities/regional_parks/blackhill
Open daily sunrise to sunset; free

Brookside Gardens
1800 Glenallen Avenue, Silver Spring, MD 20902
(301) 962-1400
www.montgomeryparks.org/brookside
Open daily sunrise to sunset; free

Cabin John Regional Park (Locust Grove Nature Center)
7777 Democracy Blvd., Bethesda, MD 20817
(301) 299-1990
www.montgomeryparks.org/facilities/regional_parks/cabinjohn
Open sunrise to sunset; free

Chesapeake & Ohio Canal National Historical Park
11710 MacArthur Boulevard, Potomac, MD 20854
(301) 767-3714
www.nps.gov/choh
Open daylight hours; fee at places

Glenview Mansion
603 Edmonston Drive, Rockville, MD 20851
(240) 314-8660
www.rockvillemd.gov
Open dawn to dusk; free

McCrillis Gardens
6910 Greentree Road, Bethesda, MD 20817
(301) 962-1455
www.montgomeryparks.org/brookside/mccrillis_gardens.shtm
Open daily 10 AM–sunset; free

McKee-Beshers Wildlife Management Area
16778 River Road, Poolesville, MD 20837
(410) 260-8540
www.dnr.state.md.us/wildlife/publiclands/central/mckeebeshers.asp
Open sunrise to sunset; free

Rock Creek Regional Park (Meadowside Nature Center)
6700 Needwood Road, Derwood, MD 20855
(301) 948-5053
www.montgomeryparks.org/facilities/regional_parks/rockcreek
Open daily sunrise to sunset; free

Seneca Creek State Park
11950 Clopper Road, Gaithersburg, MD 20878
(301) 924-2127
www.dnr.state.md.us/publiclands/central/seneca.asp
Open March–Oct., 8 AM–sunset; Nov.–Feb., 10 AM–sunset; fee on weekends

Prince George's County

Fort Washington Park
13551 Fort Washington Road, Fort Washington, MD 20744
(301) 763-4600
www.nps.gov/fowa
Open 8 AM–sunset (park); April–Oct., 9 AM–5 PM, rest of year, 9 AM–4 PM (Visitor Center and fort); $

Merkle Wildlife Sanctuary
11704 Fenno Road, Upper Marlboro, MD 20772
(301) 888-1377
www.dnr.state.md.us/publiclands/southern/merkle.asp
Open 7 AM–sunset; free

Montpelier Mansion

9650 Muirkirk Road, Laurel, MD 20708

(301) 377-7817

www.pgparks.com/sites_and_museums/MontpielierMansion.htm

Open Thur.–Tues., 11 AM–3 PM (self-guided tours); grounds open dawn to dusk; $

Oxon Hill Manor

6901 Oxon Hill Road, Fort Washington, MD 20745

(301) 839-7782

www.pgparks.com/sites_and_museums/Oxon_Hill_Manor.htm

Open Mon., 1 PM–4 PM, Tues.–Fri., 9 AM–4 PM; free

Patuxent Research Refuge

10901 Scarlet Tanager Loop, Laurel, MD 20708

(301) 497-5580

www.fws.gov/northeast/refuge/patuxent

Open sunrise to 4:30 PM daily; $

Patuxent River Park

16000 Croom Airport Road, Upper Marlboro, MD 20772

(301) 627-6074

www.pgparks.com/Things_To_Do/Nature/Patuxent_River_Park.htm

Open 8 AM–dusk; $

Riversdale House Museum

4811 Riverdale Road, Riverdale, MD 20737

(301) 864-0420

www.pgparks.com/sites_and_museums/Riversdale_House_Museum.htm

Open Mon.–Fri., 9 AM–5 PM (Visitor Center) $; grounds until dusk

Queen Anne's County

Adkins Arboretum

12610 Eveland Road, Ridgely, MD 21660

(410) 634-2847

www.adkinsarboretum.org

Open Tues.–Sat., 10 AM–4 PM, Sun., noon–4 PM; $

Washington College-Virginia Gent Decker Arboretum

300 Washington Avenue, Chestertown, MD 21620

(410) 778-2800

www.washcoll.edu

Open daily; free

Wye Island Natural Resources Management Area

632 Wye Island Road, Queenstown, MD 21658

(410) 827-7577

www.dnr.state.md.us/publiclands/eastern/wyeisland.asp

Open sunrise to sunset; free

St. Mary's County

Historic St. Mary's City

18751 Hogaboom Lane, St. Mary's City, MD 20686

(240) 895-4990

www.stmaryscity.org

Open seasonal hours; Visitor Center, Tues.–Fri., 10 AM–5 PM in winter; living history exhibits closed for the winter; grounds open year-round; $

Sotterley Plantation

44300 Sotterley Lane, Hollywood, MD 20636

(301) 373-2280

www.sotterley.org

Open Tues.–Sat., 10 AM–4 PM; $

Washington County

Antietam National Battlefield

5831 Dunker Church Road, Sharpsburg, MD 21782
(301) 432-5124
www.nps.gov/anti
Open 8:30 AM–5 PM (Visitor Center) grounds open daylight hours; $

Worcester County

Assateague State Park

6915 Stephen Decatur Highway, Berlin, MD 21811
(410) 641-2918
www.dnr.state.md.us/publiclands/eastern/assateague.asp
Open 7 AM–sunset; $

Adkins Arboretum, "History of Adkins Arboretum," www. adkinsarboretum.org.

Ann Marie Sculpture Garden & Arts Center, "The Annmarie Collection," "Works from the Hirshhorn Museum & Sculpture Garden," www. annmariegarden.org.

Audubon Naturalist Society, "Woodend Nature Sanctuary," "Woodend," www.audubonnaturalist.org.

Baltimore Museum of Art, "Collection," "BMA Sculpture Garden Audio Tour," www.artmba.org.

Blackwater National Wildlife Refuge, "Wildlife & Habitat," "About the Refuge," www.fws.gov/blackwater.

Callcott, Margaret Law, *Mistress of Riversdale: The Plantation Letters of Rosalie Stier Calvert, 1795–1821* (Baltimore, MD; Johns Hopkins University Press, 1991).

Chapman State Park, "Welcome," "A Survey of Rare Natural Heritage Resources Along Three Trails at Chapman State Park, Charles County, Maryland," "History of Mount Aventine," www.friendsofchapmansp.org/files/ChapmanTrailSurveyRodSimmons2009.pdf.

Cylburn Arboretum Association, "History," "Gardens," www.cylburn.org.

Evergreen Museum & Library, "The Garrett Family," www.museums. jhu.edu/evergreen.php.

Glenview Mansion, "Glenview Mansion at Rockville Civic Center Park." www.rockvillemd.gov/DocumentCenter/View/199.

Grear, Michael J., "The Brighton Azalea Gardens,"Brighton Dam Azalea Garden," *Journal American Rhododendron Society*, Winter 1990, Volume 44, Number 1, Virginia Tech Digital Library and Archives, http://scholar.lib.vt.edu/ejournals/JARS.

Historic London Town and Gardens, "History." "Archaeology," "Ornamental Gardens," "Woodland Garden," www. historiclondontown.org.

Historic St. Mary's City, "Plan Your Visit," www.hsmcdigshistory.org.

Howard Peters Rawlings Conservatory and Botanic Gardens, "Explore the Conservatory," "History," www.rawlingsconservatory.org.

Ladew Topiary Gardens, "Manor House-History," "History of the Gardens," www.ladewgardens.com.

Maryland Department of Natural Resources, Maryland's Natural Areas, "Battle Creek Cypress Swamp," Cranesville Swamp," www.dnr. state.md.us/wildlife/publiclands/natural_areas.

Maryland Department of Natural Resources, State Park Directory, "Assateague," "Calvert Cliffs," "Chapman," "Cunningham Falls State Park," "Deep Creek," "Gathland," "Merkle," "Rocky Gap," "Seneca Creek," "Swallow Falls State Park," "Tawes Garden," "Washington Monument," "Wye Island" www.dnr2.maryland. gov/Publiclands.

Maryland Department of Natural Resources, Wildlife and Heritage Service, "McKee-Beshers WMA," www.dnr.state.md.us/wildlife/publiclands/wmacentral.asp.

Montgomery County Department of Parks, Parks Directory, "Black Hill Regional Park," "Brookside Gardens," "Cabin John Regional Park," "McCrillis Gardens," "Rock Creek Regional Park," www.montgomeryparks.org.

Mount Harmon Plantation, "History and Preservation," "Tours and Visitor Information," www.mountharmon.org.

National Park Service, Explore This Park, "Antietam," "Chesapeake & Ohio Canal," "Fort McHenry," Fort Washington," "Hampton," "Monocacy," www.nps.gov.

Nature Conservancy, Maryland/DC, Places We Protect, "Battlecreek Cypress Swamp," "Cranesville Swamp," "Finzel Swamp," www.nature.org/ourinitiatives.

Prince George's County Department of Parks and Recreation, Sites and Museums, "Montpelier Mansion," "Oxon Hill Manor," "Patuxent River Park," "Riversdale House Museum," www.history.pgparks.com/sites_and_museums.htm, www.pgelegantsettings.com.

Reimer, Susan, "Annmarie Garden: a Southern Maryland Gem," *The Baltimore Sun*, July 15, 2010, http://articles.baltimoresun.com/2010-07-15/travel/bs-ae-travel-story-0716-20100715_1_sculpture-garden-annmarie-garden-francis-koenig.

Sherwood Gardens, "Sherwood Gardens," www.guilfordassociation.org.

Sotterley Plantation, "Colonial Revival Gardens at Historic Sotterley Plantation," "The History of Sotterley Plantation," www.sotterleyplantation.com.

Sugarloaf Mountain, "Mountain Facts," "History," www.sugarloafmd.com.

U.S. Fish & Wildlife Service, "Patuxent Research Refuge," www.fws.gov/northeast/patuxent.

Washington College, "Washington College Dedicates its New Arboretum to Mrs. Virginia Gent Decker," www.elm.washcoll.edu/past/070/04/70_4was.php.

William Paca House and Garden, "The Paca House," www.annapolis.org.